Mastering Bitcoin and Cryptocurrencies: A Comprehensive Guide for Beginners

TABLE OF CONTENTS

I. Introduction

II. Bitcoin – Pioneer of Cryptocurrencies

A. The Birth of Bitcoin and Its Evolution

B. The Lightning Network

C. Using Bitcoin as a Store of Value

D. Future Perspectives for Bitcoin

III. Altcoins - Alternative Cryptocurrencies

A. Introduction to Altcoins

B. Major Altcoins and Their Characteristics

C. Classification of Cryptocurrencies

D. Specific Uses of Altcoins

E. Comparison with Bitcoin and Other Major Cryptocurrencies

F. Security of Bitcoin and Cryptocurrencies

G. Growth Potential

IV. Smart Investment: Dollar-Cost Averaging in Cryptocurrencies

A. Principle of DCA and Why It's Useful for Cryptocurrency Investment

B. How to Implement an Effective DCA Plan

C. Concrete Examples and Simulations to Illustrate Potential Gains with DCA

V. Taking Profits in a Bull Market

A. Why It's Important to Regularly Take Profits

B. How to Set a Realistic Profit Target

C. Strategies for Gradually Selling Cryptocurrencies

VI. Investing in Solid Projects and Diversifying Your Portfolio

A. How to Identify Solid Projects and Avoid Scams

B. Why Diversifying Your Portfolio Is Important for Risk Reduction

C. Tips for Allocating Your Capital Among Different Cryptocurrencies and Projects

D. Do Your Own Research Before Investing in a Cryptocurrency

E. Investments in ICOs and STOs

F. Avoid Impulsive Investments, Don't Succumb to Market Panic or Excitement, and Make Informed Decisions

G. Be Patient, Long-Term Investments Generally Yield Better Returns Than Short-Term Investments

VII. Managing Emotions and Avoiding Psychological Traps

A. Major Psychological Traps Faced by Cryptocurrency Investors B. How to Manage Emotions and Avoid Making Impulsive Decisions

C. Tips for Maintaining a Healthy and Optimistic Mindset Despite Market Fluctuations

D. Don't Bet More Than You Can Afford to Lose

E. Understanding Market Cycle Psychology

F. Market Manipulation

VIII. Following News and Market Trends

A. Why It's Important to Follow News and Market Trends

B. How to Stay Informed and Identify Investment Opportunities

C. Tips for Avoiding Fake News and Unreliable Information Sources

D. Use Reliable Exchange Platforms: Choose Reputable Platforms to Avoid Scams and Hacks

IX. Emerging Trends in the World of Cryptocurrencies : Perspectives and Narratives for the Future

A. Institutional Adoption

B. Development of CBDCs

C. Integration of Blockchain in Traditional Sectors

D. Development of DeFi

E. Digital Identity

F. Real World Assets

X. Bonus : The Guide to Thoughtful Investment

XI. The Final Word.

Dear Cryptophiles,

This book is dedicated to you, the enthusiasts and passionate individuals who explore the mysteries of the cryptocurrency universe with enthusiasm and determination. Dive into these pages to discover the keys that unlock the doors of this captivating ecosystem where the revolutionary technology of blockchain meets the financial opportunities of the future. Prepare to embrace change and shape your digital future, for this adventure is for you, the visionaries of the new financial era.

Cryptolove, Mike

For real-time updates on Bitcoin and cryptocurrencies, follow me on X (formerly Twitter: @mickael_81)

MikeCryptoInvest

I. Introduction

In 2019, I discovered a fascinating universe – that of cryptocurrencies. It all started with a series of online articles and discussions about Bitcoin and other Altcoins. Initially, I didn't fully grasp the concept, but I sensed there was something unique and revolutionary about this idea of digital currency. What attracted me the most was the underlying technology, blockchain, with its enormous potential to revolutionize the financial industry.

I began devouring everything I could find on the subject. I joined online forums, watched YouTube videos at double speed, followed domain experts on social media, and started grasping the fundamental principles of cryptocurrencies. I was fascinated by the potential of this emerging technology.

Driven by my curiosity and enthusiasm for cryptocurrencies, I decided to take my first steps as an investor. I invested in several cryptocurrency projects, drawn by their potential and promises of high returns. However, like any novice investor, I made mistakes.

My initial experiences with cryptocurrency investment were quite turbulent. I faced losses, sometimes significant ones, but I considered each failure a valuable lesson. I learned to conduct thorough research on projects before investing, understand the risks associated with each investment, and develop a long-term investment strategy.

Furthermore, I learned to manage my portfolio to minimize risks. I diversified my investments, spreading my capital among multiple projects to reduce the impact of volatility in any single project on my overall portfolio. I also learned to be patient, resist the temptation to sell during temporary market downturns, and wait for the realization of my long-term investment goals.

The years 2019 and 2020 were particularly challenging for cryptocurrency investors. The market experienced significant price declines, and many panicked and sold their investments out of fear of further losses. For me, however, these periods of decline were opportunities to learn and deepen my understanding of the cryptocurrency market.

During these market downturns, I spent a lot of time studying and understanding the dynamics of the cryptocurrency market. I analyzed the factors influencing cryptocurrency prices and learned to identify signs of market recovery.

These downturns also gave me the opportunity to identify new promising projects. I used this time to conduct in-depth research on various projects, looking for those with the potential to generate high long-term returns.

Today, I am proud of my investments and the gains I have made in the cryptocurrency market. The lessons I've learned, the skills I've acquired, and the patience I've demonstrated have paid off. I have succeeded in making profitable investments and increasing my capital.

Having gained valuable experience and in-depth knowledge in the field of cryptocurrencies, I decided to share what I have learned with others. I began actively participating in forums, meetings, and sharing my advice with those interested in cryptocurrency investment.

It is this desire to share and contribute to the cryptocurrency community that led me to the idea of writing this book. By sharing my experiences, failures, and successes, I hope to help other investors navigate the complex world of cryptocurrencies.

The cryptocurrency market is constantly evolving. New projects emerge every day, and old ones continue to grow and adapt. It is an exciting and dynamic field, offering many opportunities for those willing to learn and adapt.

I firmly believe that anyone can succeed in cryptocurrency investment. It requires patience, caution, and a willingness to invest in solid and promising projects. It is also essential to stay informed and continue learning, as the cryptocurrency market is constantly evolving.

With this book, I hope to contribute to the cryptocurrency investor community by sharing my knowledge and helping others succeed in this fascinating market.

II. Bitcoin – Pioneer of Cryptocurrencies

A. The Birth of Bitcoin and Its Evolution

The story of Bitcoin is fascinating, full of twists and turns and developments that have shaped the rise of this revolutionary cryptocurrency. Let's go back to the origins of Bitcoin and explore its journey up to the present day.

The story of Bitcoin begins in 2008 when the mysterious identity known as Satoshi Nakamoto published a document titled "Bitcoin: A Peer-to-Peer Electronic Cash System" on a cryptographic mailing list. This document laid the groundwork for a new concept: a decentralized digital currency that could function without the intervention of a central authority.

The number of tokens available for Bitcoin is fixed at 21 million. This is one of the fundamental features that distinguish Bitcoin from traditional currencies and other cryptocurrencies. This limit of 21 million was integrated into the Bitcoin protocol from its creation by its mysterious creator, Satoshi Nakamoto.

The limitation to 21 million bitcoins is intrinsically linked to the mining process, which is the means by which new bitcoins are created and added to circulation.

In January 2009, the Bitcoin network was launched with the creation of the first block, called the "genesis block," thus marking the beginning of the Bitcoin blockchain. Early users began mining bitcoins and conducting transactions. Initially, Bitcoin was mainly used by a small circle of cryptography enthusiasts.

Bitcoin mining is the process by which new bitcoins are created and network transactions are verified and secured. It is an essential activity for the functioning of the network.

Mining relies on special computers called "miners" that use their computing power to solve complex mathematical problems. These problems are known as "proofs of work" and are designed to be difficult to solve but easy to verify once found.

Miners gather pending transactions into blocks and then attempt to find the solution to the proof-of-work problem for that block. The first miner to solve the problem and find the solution is rewarded with a fixed amount of newly created bitcoins, as well as the transaction fees associated with the transactions included in the block.

Once a block is solved, it is added to the blockchain, which is the public and immutable database that records all bitcoin transactions. Each block is linked to the previous one, thus forming a chain of blocks.

Bitcoin mining is a competitive process, as many miners simultaneously attempt to solve the same problem. This creates a competition to find the solution as quickly as possible. Consequently, computing power and the use of specialized equipment, such as Application-Specific Integrated Circuits (ASICs), have become essential to be competitive in Bitcoin mining.

Initially, when the Bitcoin network was launched in 2009, miners were rewarded with a certain amount of bitcoins for each block of transactions they verified and added to the blockchain. This gradually distributed the newly created bitcoins in the network.

However, this reward halves approximately every four years in an event called "halving." The number of bitcoins created with each mined block is halved during each halving. This means that the creation of new bitcoins slows down over time and will eventually reach a point where the total number of bitcoins cannot increase any further.

This is programmed into the Bitcoin code to maintain a limited and predictable supply of bitcoins over time. The next halving event is scheduled for April-May 2024.

This supply limitation contributes to Bitcoin's perception as a potentially valuable store of value. Unlike fiat currencies, which can be printed in unlimited quantities by central banks, Bitcoin is subject to predetermined and immutable scarcity. This scarcity is one of the factors that have contributed to sparking investor interest and fueling discussions about the "digital" nature of gold.

In October 2009, the first Bitcoin/dollar exchange rate was established, allowing people to buy and sell bitcoins for traditional currencies. This was the first time a value was assigned to it: 0.001 dollar. This value was set based on the cost of electrical production needed to generate one unit by a computer.

During the early years, Bitcoin remained relatively obscure and unknown to the general public.

On May 22, 2010, American developer Laszlo Hanyecz made a historic transaction by spending 10,000 bitcoins to buy two pizzas. At that time, Bitcoin was of interest to technology enthusiasts but was not yet used to purchase real goods. Laszlo Hanyecz posted a message on the specialized Bitcoin Talk forum, proposing: "I'll pay 10,000 bitcoins for a couple of pizzas, like two large ones, so I have some left for the next day. If you're interested, let me know so we can arrange it." Four days later, he thanked a British user who had ordered him two pizzas by calling the Papa John's restaurant in Jacksonville, Florida, where Laszlo Hanyecz resided. He shared a photo as proof of his transaction.

This event is now famous as the "Bitcoin Pizza." It is often cited to illustrate how the perception of Bitcoin's value has evolved over the years. The 10,000 bitcoins that Laszlo Hanyecz spent on those pizzas are worth a considerable sum today, given Bitcoin's meteoric price growth over time. This anecdote serves as a reminder of both Bitcoin's humble beginnings as a medium of exchange and its rise as a valuable digital asset.

In 2011, Bitcoin began to attract media attention following its use on underground online markets, such as Silk Road, where bitcoins were used for illegal transactions. This visibility contributed to Bitcoin's growing popularity, although its association with criminal activities also raised concerns.

In 2013, the price of Bitcoin experienced a sharp increase, reaching unprecedented highs ($1,152 on December 5, 2013). This attracted the attention of investors and speculators, who saw Bitcoin as a lucrative investment opportunity. However, this speculative bubble eventually burst, leading to a significant decline in the price of Bitcoin.

Despite this volatility, Bitcoin continued to gain popularity and attract the interest of large companies. In 2014, Microsoft became one of the first major companies to accept payments in Bitcoin. This gradual acceptance by renowned companies strengthened Bitcoin's credibility and adoption. However, a year later, Microsoft reversed course and discontinued Bitcoin payments.

On December 17, 2017, Bitcoin reached new historic highs, surpassing $19,000 per bitcoin. This rapid rise was largely due to media hype and massive interest from retail investors. However, once again, this surge was followed by a significant correction, leading to a prolonged period of price declines.

From 2020 onwards, Bitcoin's story has been marked by numerous significant events and developments.

In 2020, Bitcoin experienced significant volatility due to the global COVID-19 pandemic. At the beginning of the year, the price of Bitcoin dropped significantly to around $5,000, much like global financial markets. However, it quickly rebounded and reached new historic highs by the end of the year.

In May 2020, an event called the "halving" occurred on the Bitcoin network. Every four years, the reward for Bitcoin miners is halved. This reduces Bitcoin's inflation and adjusts the available supply in the market. The 2020 halving generated great interest and was considered a potential factor in price increases.

Throughout 2020, more and more traditional financial institutions showed increasing interest in Bitcoin. Companies like MicroStrategy and Square announced massive investments in Bitcoin, considering the cryptocurrency as an alternative store of value.

In December 2020, the price of Bitcoin reached a historic high exceeding $20,000, fueled by growing demand from institutional investors and individuals. This bullish trend continued into 2021.

In February 2021, Elon Musk, the founder of Tesla and SpaceX, announced that Tesla had purchased $1.5 billion worth of Bitcoin and would accept Bitcoin payments for Tesla car purchases. This announcement contributed to a significant increase in the price of Bitcoin and greater adoption by large companies.

However, in the spring of 2021, the cryptocurrency market experienced a major correction. The price of Bitcoin and other cryptocurrencies saw a dramatic decline, losing more than half of its value compared to the historic high. Several factors contributed to this correction, including environmental concerns related to Bitcoin mining energy consumption and profit-taking by investors after a period of steep price increases.

Coinbase is one of the leading cryptocurrency exchange platforms in the world. In April 2021, it became the first major cryptocurrency-related company to go public on the NASDAQ, a major American stock exchange. This IPO was seen as a pivotal moment for the cryptocurrency sector, as it further legitimized digital currencies by integrating them into the traditional financial world.

Coinbase's public offering generated great interest from investors and the general public. Coinbase's shares were listed under the symbol "COIN," and their performance was closely monitored. However, like any publicly traded company, the value of Coinbase's shares was subject to fluctuations in the stock market and overall cryptocurrency market conditions.

Cryptocurrencies are complex. The excitement surrounding Coinbase's IPO may have contributed to an initial increase in cryptocurrency prices, but it may also have created temporary overvaluation. Subsequently, some investors may have taken profits, leading to downward pressure on prices.

In response to environmental concerns, there has been increasing attention to the environmental impact of Bitcoin mining, leading to discussions on the need to develop more sustainable mining methods and initiatives to reduce the carbon footprint of the Bitcoin network.

Despite price fluctuations and challenges, Bitcoin has continued to gain adoption and recognition. More and more large companies and financial institutions have started integrating Bitcoin into their operations and exploring opportunities offered by blockchain technology.

In September 2021, El Salvador became the first country in the world to officially adopt Bitcoin as legal tender. This historic decision was announced by President Nayib Bukele and took effect on September 7,

2021.

El Salvador's adoption of Bitcoin was formalized through the Bitcoin Law, which declared that Bitcoin would be used as legal tender alongside the US dollar, which was already the country's official currency. This means that businesses are required to accept Bitcoin as a means of payment, and citizens have the option to pay their taxes and other obligations in Bitcoin.

To facilitate the adoption and use of Bitcoin, the Salvadoran government also launched a mobile application called "Chivo Wallet." This application allows users to store, receive, and send bitcoins. As part of the initiative, every Salvadoran citizen also received $30 worth of Bitcoin when the system was implemented.

The government also installed Bitcoin ATMs throughout the country, called "Chivo ATMs," allowing users to convert their bitcoins into US dollars or vice versa.

The stated goal of this decision was to stimulate financial inclusion, encourage technological innovation, and facilitate cross-border fund transfers for Salvadoran citizens, especially those without access to traditional banking services.

However, this decision has sparked mixed reactions both domestically and internationally. Some applaud the initiative as a step toward financial decentralization and economic autonomy, while others express concerns about Bitcoin's volatility, the lack of clear regulation, and the potential implications on the national economy.

It is also worth noting that El Salvador's adoption of Bitcoin has had a significant impact on the Bitcoin market, as the Salvadoran government purchased bitcoins to build up a reserve worth several hundred million dollars.

It is important to closely monitor El Salvador's experience with Bitcoin, as it could potentially influence the decisions of other countries regarding cryptocurrencies and digital currencies in the future.

The possibilities offered by blockchain technology in areas such as finance, logistics, and data management are generating significant interest and giving rise to many innovative projects.

In 2022, Bitcoin continued to gain recognition and adoption. More and more companies, including tech giants and financial institutions, began integrating Bitcoin into their operations. This increased adoption was supported by the growing perception of Bitcoin as a viable asset class and an alternative store of value.

An important development in 2022 was the expansion of the Bitcoin futures market. More exchanges and financial institutions introduced Bitcoin-related derivative products, allowing institutional investors to take positions on Bitcoin without actually holding the cryptocurrency.

On July 24, 2023, Elon Musk decided to rebrand Twitter as "X" with the aim of transforming the social media platform into a versatile application similar to "WeChat" in China. His goal is to create an ecosystem within "X" where users can engage in various activities in addition to social interactions. In this new direction, Musk plans to integrate cryptocurrency payments within the "X" platform.

Among the cryptocurrencies considered for payments are Bitcoin, Ethereum, and Dogecoin. These digital currencies are well positioned to play a crucial role in "X"'s payment system.

In this regard, on August 29, 2023, Elon Musk obtained a currency transmission license from Rhode Island. This license is required for anyone or entity handling virtual currency or conducting virtual currency transactions on behalf of others, according to the regulations of the Rhode Island Department of Business Regulation.

By obtaining this license, "X" would be authorized to implement cryptocurrency payments on its platform, which could pave the way for services such as storage, transfer, and exchange of cryptocurrencies. This initiative reflects Musk's ambitions to further develop the use of cryptocurrencies in transactions and value exchange within an extensive social platform.

On the same day, the US Court of Appeals for the DC Circuit ruled in favor of Grayscale in a dispute against the SEC, significantly enhancing the prospects for approval of a Bitcoin Exchange-Traded Fund (ETF).

Previously, the SEC had rejected Grayscale's request to transform its Grayscale Bitcoin Trust into an ETF.

The key issue for the SEC lay in rejecting a Spot Bitcoin ETF over the past few years, citing the lack of a sufficiently large regulated market to prevent manipulation. However, the court pointed out the SEC's previous approval for a Bitcoin product based on futures contracts. The court argued that futures markets and spot markets are "similar" products, so if one is approved, the other should be too.

The court highlighted the interconnectedness between Bitcoin futures and spot markets, noting that manipulation in one can affect futures contract prices. As a result, the court criticized the SEC's decision quite openly, stating that its refusal to approve Grayscale's proposal was arbitrary and capricious, due to the lack of a coherent explanation for the differential treatment of similar products.

However, despite this decision in favor of Grayscale, concerns related to market manipulation have not been dismissed. The court did not alleviate these concerns but rather pointed out an inconsistency in the SEC's decision. This situation has sparked discussions about the need to clarify approval criteria for cryptocurrency-related ETFs.

Among the candidates for a Spot Bitcoin ETF are various names such as Grayscale Bitcoin Trust, Ark/21 Bitcoin Trust, Bitwise Bitcoin ETF Trust, BlackRock Bitcoin ETF Trust, Bitcoin VanEck ETF Trust, WisdomTree Bitcoin Trust, Valkyrie Bitcoin Fund, Invesco Galaxy Bitcoin ETF, and Fidelity Wise Origin Bitcoin Trust.

It is now highly likely that the SEC will authorize these Spot Bitcoin ETFs in early 2024. The approval of a Spot Bitcoin ETF would have several significant consequences for the cryptocurrency market and the entire financial landscape.

Here are some of the main potential consequences:

Increased Accessibility: A Bitcoin spot ETF would allow investors to access the Bitcoin market more easily and traditionally, through their usual brokerage accounts. This would eliminate the need to directly hold and secure Bitcoins, which could attract new investors.

- **Increased Legitimacy:** Approval of a Bitcoin ETF by regulators would strengthen Bitcoin's legitimacy as a recognized asset class. This would send a positive signal to institutional investors and major players in the financial market, who may be more inclined to get involved in the sector.

- **Capital Flows:** The Bitcoin ETF could attract considerable capital, as institutional and retail investors could invest in Bitcoin without having to directly manage the technical aspects of holding cryptocurrencies. This could potentially increase demand for Bitcoin and positively influence prices.

- **Potential Volatility:** While approval of an ETF could bring some stability to the market, it could also intensify volatility. Bitcoin price fluctuations could be amplified by massive inflows and outflows of investments related to the ETF.

- **Increased Monitoring:** ETFs are regulated by the SEC, which would involve regular monitoring of ETF Bitcoin-related activity. This could lead to better market transparency and increased monitoring of potentially manipulative practices.

- **Impact on Derivative Markets:** The existence of a Bitcoin Spot ETF could influence futures markets and Bitcoin-related derivative contracts. Futures prices and positions could be influenced by investment flows into the ETF.

- **Influence on General Perception:** Approval of a Bitcoin ETF could influence public opinion in general, attracting more attention and interest in cryptocurrencies as a viable asset class.
- **Impact on Regulation :** Approval of a Bitcoin Spot ETF could encourage other companies to file similar applications, which could influence cryptocurrency and digital asset regulation as a whole.

B. The Lightning Network

Bitcoin regulation has also continued to evolve. Many countries have been working on establishing a regulatory framework for cryptocurrencies, seeking to protect investors and prevent illicit activities. Some countries have taken a favorable approach to cryptocurrencies, while others have imposed stricter restrictions.

Meanwhile, the development of the Lightning Network, a second-layer scaling technology for the Bitcoin network, has continued to progress.

The Lightning Network is somewhat like a fast lane for Bitcoin payments. Imagine you want to send Bitcoin to a friend, but you want it to be really quick and cheap. The Lightning Network allows you to do this by avoiding directly congesting the Bitcoin blockchain.

It's like you're opening a little private channel with your friend. You deposit some Bitcoin into this channel. Now you and your friend can send payments back and forth to each other as much as you want, almost instantly and with very low fees, without every transaction being recorded on the main Bitcoin blockchain.

When you're done, you can close this channel, and the final balance is recorded on the Bitcoin blockchain. This saves time and fees while still maintaining overall blockchain security. The Lightning Network makes Bitcoin transactions faster and more efficient while helping to unclog the main network.

Here are some key points regarding the development of the Lightning Network during this period :

- ❖ **Network Expansion:** The Lightning network has continued to grow with the addition of new nodes and payment channels. More and more users have begun exploring the possibilities offered by this technology, allowing for faster and cheaper transactions than on the main Bitcoin chain.

- ❖ **User Experience Improvements:** Progress has been made to make using the Lightning Network more user-friendly and accessible to users. New applications and wallets have been developed to simplify the process of opening channels, routing payments, and managing funds on the Lightning network.

- ❖ **Increasing Adoption** : The number of merchants and service providers accepting payments via the Lightning Network has increased. This has allowed users to spend their bitcoins more easily on everyday goods and services, creating a true economy based on the Lightning Network.

- ❖ **Integration with Other Networks** : The Lightning Network has begun exploring interoperability opportunities with other cryptocurrency networks. Initiatives have been launched to enable atomic swaps between different chains, which would facilitate cross-border transactions and broader adoption of this technology.

- ❖ **Experimentation with New Features** : Lightning Network developers have explored new features and capabilities, such as private payments and smart contracts. These developments aim to expand the use cases of the Lightning Network and improve transaction privacy.

- ❖ **Collaboration and Research** : Collaboration efforts between developers, researchers, and communities have continued to support the development of the Lightning Network. Research initiatives have been launched to solve specific problems, such as payment routing and channel management, to improve the efficiency and reliability of the network.

- ❖ **Education and Awareness** : Industry players and enthusiast communities have organized events, workshops, and education campaigns to further raise awareness among potential users about the benefits of the Lightning Network and to foster its adoption.

The Lightning Network continued to make progress in 2023 with increasing adoption, user experience improvements, and experimentation with new features. The development of this technology is essential for addressing Bitcoin network scaling issues and making transactions faster, cheaper, and more accessible to a larger number of users.

C. Use of Bitcoin as a Store of Value

Bitcoin has evolved over time to become much more than just a digital currency; it has also become an attractive store of value for many investors and institutions worldwide. This evolution is due to several unique characteristics of Bitcoin, including its programmed scarcity, resistance to censorship, and decentralization.

Concrete examples of the use of Bitcoin as a store of value abound in the financial world. Some publicly traded companies, such as MicroStrategy and Tesla, have allocated a significant portion of their treasury reserves to Bitcoin. MicroStrategy even issued bonds to finance its Bitcoin acquisitions. This trend has been followed by other companies, indicating growing confidence in Bitcoin as a strong reserve asset.

Wealth managers and institutional investors have also begun to view Bitcoin as a hedge against inflation and currency fluctuations. Concerns about fiat currency instability and accommodative monetary policies have led to the adoption of Bitcoin as a more resilient alternative. Investment funds such as Grayscale Bitcoin Trust have facilitated institutional access to Bitcoin by offering managed exposure to this digital asset.

The use of Bitcoin as a store of value is also widespread in countries where local currencies are prone to extreme volatility or economic governance issues. In these regions, Bitcoin can act as a hedge against the devaluation of the local currency. For example, in Venezuela and Argentina, where hyperinflation has had a significant impact on local economies, more and more people are turning to Bitcoin to preserve the value of their assets.

Finally, Bitcoin is often compared to digital gold due to its fixed scarcity and durability as a store of value. Like gold, Bitcoin can serve as a means of capital preservation during periods of economic turmoil or global financial crisis. This comparison has led to increased institutional and individual demand for Bitcoin as a reserve asset.

The increasing use of Bitcoin as a store of value has become a significant trend in the global financial landscape. From companies to individual investors to countries grappling with monetary issues, Bitcoin is establishing itself as a credible and modern alternative for preserving value across diverse economic environments.

D. Future Outlook for Bitcoin

Bitcoin, since its humble beginnings in 2009, has evolved dramatically to become a major disruptive force in the global financial landscape. As we examine the future outlook for Bitcoin, it is important to recognize the elements that have contributed to its current success and to explore the trends that could influence its long-term trajectory.

One of the most intriguing prospects for Bitcoin is its potential as a digital store of value. As more and more individuals and institutions recognize the benefits of Bitcoin as a hedge against inflation, currency volatility, and economic uncertainty, its role as a digital gold could become even more pronounced.

Additionally, as technological advancements continue to improve scalability and usability, Bitcoin could become more accessible and user-friendly, attracting a broader range of users and investors.

If Bitcoin manages to solidify this position as a store of value, it could become an essential component of diverse investors' portfolios.

Bitcoin could also play a significant role in democratizing access to financial services globally. In regions where access to traditional banking services is limited, Bitcoin offers an alternative for the unbanked or underserved. By enabling fast and inexpensive cross-border transactions, Bitcoin could help reduce barriers to international trade and enhance financial inclusion.

Technological innovation is another pillar of Bitcoin's future prospects. The continuous development of solutions like the Lightning Network enables instant and low-cost Bitcoin transactions, which can enhance user experience and increase adoption. Moreover, Bitcoin's integration with emerging technologies like decentralized finance (DeFi) could further expand its utility, allowing for lending, borrowing, and other financial activities without intermediaries.

However, it's essential to recognize the challenges Bitcoin faces. Regulatory issues, price volatility, and environmental concerns surround Bitcoin and may influence its future trajectory. Integrating Bitcoin into the traditional financial system could also lead to tensions between the need for regulation and the desire to preserve Bitcoin's decentralized characteristics.

Overall, Bitcoin's future prospects are imbued with uncertainties and opportunities. As it continues to evolve and grow, Bitcoin could play a significant role in transforming global financial systems, setting new investment standards, and promoting global financial inclusion. The path ahead will undoubtedly be complex, but Bitcoin's history so far has shown its resilience and ability to defy expectations. The coming years could see Bitcoin playing an even more central role in how we conceive and interact with finance and technology.

Although Bitcoin is the most well-known and popular cryptocurrency, it's important to note that there is a whole universe of cryptocurrencies offering a variety of features and applications.

III. Altcoins - Alternative Cryptocurrencies

A. Introduction to Altcoins

The world of cryptocurrencies is much broader than just Bitcoin. Alongside this first cryptocurrency that paved the way, many Altcoins have emerged, offering a fascinating diversity of alternatives and innovations. Altcoins are cryptocurrencies alternative to Bitcoin, each with its own characteristics, objectives, and specific use cases.

In this introduction, we delve into the captivating universe of Altcoins, discovering their essential role in the cryptocurrency ecosystem. While Bitcoin led the way as a pioneer, cryptocurrencies quickly became key players, bringing new features, innovative approaches, and exciting opportunities, ready to tackle new challenges. Among these challenges, the "trilemma" emerges as a crucial concept to understand.

By balancing the imperatives of **security**, **decentralization**, and **scalability**, blockchain projects must navigate carefully to achieve an optimal balance :

- ❖ **Security :** Security is paramount in the world of cryptocurrencies and blockchains. Networks must be protected against malicious attacks, fraud, and hacking. A secure architecture ensures that transactions and data stored on the blockchain are immutable and inviolable.

- **Decentralization** : Decentralization entails that control and decision-making are not centralized in the hands of a single entity. In cryptocurrencies, decentralization is essential to avoid single points of failure and to ensure that the network cannot be manipulated or censored by a single party.

- **Scalability** : Scalability concerns a blockchain's ability to handle a large number of transactions quickly and efficiently, without sacrificing security and decentralization. As cryptocurrency adoption increases, it's important for networks to handle the growing demand without slowing down or becoming less secure.

However, the challenge of the trilemma lies in the fact that these three objectives are often in conflict with each other. For example, increasing scalability by increasing transaction processing capacity can sometimes compromise decentralization, as it may require the use of more powerful and centralized network nodes. Similarly, improving security by making consensus stricter can slow down scalability.

Many blockchain platforms attempt to strike a balance between these three objectives by adopting different technological approaches. For example, Ethereum explores scaling solutions like Ethereum 2.0 and sidechains to improve scalability while maintaining an acceptable level of security and decentralization.

Each cryptocurrency has its own identity and value proposition, offering users and investors a multitude of options.

In this chapter, we will explore some of the top Altcoins that have made their presence felt in the cryptocurrency space. We will discover their distinctive features, such as their consensus protocols, mining algorithms, smart contract functionalities, governance, and much more. Altcoins such as Ethereum, Ripple, Litecoin, Cardano, Cosmos, Solana, and many others, will be highlighted to illustrate the diversity and possibilities offered by these digital alternatives.

Additionally, we will examine the specific uses of Altcoins in different sectors and use cases. We will discover how they can be used beyond simple digital currency, offering solutions in areas such as decentralized finance (DeFi), digital identities, data exchange networks, the Internet of Things (IoT), and many more. Altcoins play a crucial role in expanding the cryptocurrency ecosystem by providing tools and platforms to innovate in many sectors.

B. Major Altcoins and Their Characteristics

In this section, we dive into the world of major Altcoins that have made their presence felt in the cryptocurrency space. Each of these Altcoins offers distinctive features that set them apart from Bitcoin and give them a unique value proposition.

- ❖ **Ethereum,** launched in 2015 by developer Vitalik Buterin, is one of the most influential and innovative cryptocurrencies and blockchain platforms. Ethereum is not limited to being just a digital currency but also offers an environment for the development of smart contracts and decentralized applications (dApps).

At the heart of Ethereum is the native cryptocurrency called Ether (ETH), used to pay transaction fees on the network and incentivize miners to secure the blockchain. Ethereum initially uses the same consensus mechanism as Bitcoin, called proof of work (PoW), but plans to migrate to a proof of stake (PoS) model with Ethereum 2.0, aiming to improve scalability and energy efficiency.

The major innovation introduced by Ethereum is the ability to create smart contracts, self-executing programs that run automatically when certain predefined conditions are met. This opens up a wide range of possibilities for the development of decentralized applications, from voting systems to games to decentralized markets.

Ethereum also introduced "ERC-20 tokens", standards that allow the creation and interoperability of custom tokens on the Ethereum blockchain. These tokens have been widely used for initial coin offerings (ICOs) and have contributed to the growth of the cryptocurrency ecosystem.

The continued expansion of the Ethereum ecosystem is supported by the developer community, which actively contributes to protocol updates. However, scalability remains a challenge, and Ethereum 2.0 aims to address these issues by introducing fundamental changes in how transactions are confirmed. The major upgrade called "The Merge" was implemented on September 15, 2022, marking a significant event in recent cryptocurrency history. After a long and complex migration, Ethereum officially joined the ranks of hundreds of blockchains adopting the consensus mechanism called proof of stake (PoS).

Ethereum has also played a central role in the emergence of Decentralized Finance (DeFi), offering traditional financial services such as lending, borrowing, and trading, but in a fully decentralized manner. This has contributed to the rapid growth of the DeFi ecosystem on the Ethereum blockchain.

Although Ethereum has been at the forefront of many innovations, it faces challenges such as scalability, competition from other blockchains, and environmental issues associated with proof of work. However, with Ethereum 2.0 underway, the community is actively working on the network's future.

Ethereum has transformed how we conceive and use blockchain technology while striving to address challenges to maintain its relevance in an ever-evolving crypto landscape.

- ❖ **Ripple,** launched in 2012, is both a decentralized payment platform and a cryptocurrency called XRP. Designed to facilitate international transactions and cross-border payments, Ripple aims to address inefficiencies in the traditional financial system, particularly concerning fund transfers.

Ripple's main feature is its unique consensus protocol called "Consensus by Distributed Agreement". Unlike most other cryptocurrencies that use proof of work (PoW) or proof of stake (PoS), Ripple uses a network of validators to validate transactions, allowing for faster consensus.

XRP, Ripple's native cryptocurrency, plays a central role in the network as a means of transferring value. Unlike other cryptocurrencies, XRP is not mined. Instead, a fixed amount was pre-mined at the creation of the network, and it is managed by Ripple Labs. This contributes to the stability of the network and the predictability of supply.

Ripple positions itself as an ideal solution for financial institutions and banks due to its transaction speed (in seconds) and relatively low transaction costs. The platform offers solutions such as xCurrent (for payment processing) and xRapid (for liquidity), allowing financial institutions to conduct international payments more efficiently.

Ripple's vision is to improve the fluidity of the global financial system by facilitating cross-border payments. By collaborating with partners in the financial sector, Ripple aims to establish a global infrastructure where transactions can be conducted seamlessly, securely, and near-instantaneously.

However, Ripple has also faced regulatory challenges. In December 2020, the United States Securities and Exchange Commission (SEC) filed a lawsuit against Ripple Labs, alleging that the sale of XRP constituted an unregistered securities offering. This lawsuit has had significant repercussions on the price of XRP and has sparked debates about cryptocurrency regulation. The outcome of the lawsuit is expected in 2024.

Through its unique consensus protocol and solutions tailored for financial institutions, Ripple seeks to improve the efficiency of the global financial system despite the regulatory challenges it faces.

- ❖ **Litecoin**, launched in 2011 by Charlie Lee, is one of the earliest cryptocurrencies to emerge after Bitcoin. Designed as "digital silver," Litecoin shares many similarities with Bitcoin but also presents distinctive features.

Litecoin was created using Bitcoin's source code, with some modifications aimed at improving certain limitations. One notable difference is the faster block generation time, with a block every 2.5 minutes compared to Bitcoin's 10 minutes. This allows for faster transaction confirmations.

Litecoin's consensus protocol is also based on proof of work (PoW), similar to Bitcoin. However, it uses the Scrypt algorithm instead of SHA-256, making Litecoin mining more accessible to a larger number of miners and promoting increased decentralization.

Litecoin is often seen as complementary "digital silver" to Bitcoin's "digital gold." Its creator, Charlie Lee, aimed to create a lighter and faster cryptocurrency while maintaining Bitcoin's security and decentralization.

Litecoin's simplicity is also reflected in its network. Unlike some more complex blockchain projects, Litecoin maintains a simple and straightforward approach, focusing on its main goal of offering fast and inexpensive transactions.

Litecoin is widely accepted in the cryptocurrency ecosystem and is available on many exchange platforms. It has gained popularity as a means of online payment and is often used for small to medium-sized transactions.

Although Litecoin does not aim to revolutionize smart contracts and other advanced features, its role as a leading cryptocurrency and its stable history make it a significant player in the digital currency landscape. With faster block generation time, a Scrypt consensus algorithm, and a focus on simplicity and transaction speed, Litecoin occupies a notable place in the cryptocurrency ecosystem.

- ❖ **Cardano**, launched in 2015 by Ethereum co-founder Charles Hoskinson, is a major project in the cryptocurrency space. The project aims to create an advanced blockchain platform with a particular focus on security, scalability, and sustainability.

It was developed by IOHK (Input Output Hong Kong) in collaboration with cryptography and computer science experts. Cardano stands out for its scientific and research-based approach. It is built in layers, with a settlement layer and a computational layer. This modular design allows for increased flexibility and scalability.

Cardano's blockchain uses a consensus algorithm called Ouroboros, which is based on proof of stake (PoS). This approach aims to improve energy efficiency compared to proof of work systems while ensuring network security. Cardano also positions itself as a platform promoting decentralized governance. Its governance model allows ADA token holders (the native cryptocurrency of Cardano) to participate in important decisions regarding protocol updates, ensuring greater inclusivity in network development.

The Cardano project focuses on global financial inclusion by aiming to provide financial services to populations that currently lack access. It emphasizes creating a sustainable and scalable blockchain infrastructure to support these long-term goals.

Scientific research is at the core of Cardano's development, with a formal process of specification and verification aimed at ensuring protocol robustness. This reinforces confidence in the security of the network and smart contracts that can be executed on the platform.

The Cardano ecosystem also includes initiatives such as the "Cardano Africa" program, which aims to accelerate blockchain technology adoption in Africa, as well as collaborations with governments and organizations worldwide.

With its decentralized governance model and commitment to global financial inclusion, Cardano occupies a significant place in the cryptocurrency ecosystem by offering an innovative and well-thought-out blockchain platform.

❖ **Cosmos**, launched in 2014, is a major initiative in the blockchain and cryptocurrency space. At the core of this project is the cryptocurrency Atom, designed to power the Cosmos ecosystem. Cosmos aims to address some of the fundamental challenges facing blockchains today, including interoperability, scalability, and governance.

Interoperability is one of Cosmos' distinctive features. It offers a solution called "Hub-and-Spoke," where multiple blockchains, called zones, are connected to a central hub, called the "Cosmos Hub." This allows different blockchains to communicate with each other, creating an interoperable ecosystem.

Scalability is also at the heart of Cosmos' concerns. The platform uses an approach called "Tendermint," a Byzantine Fault Tolerant (BFT) consensus algorithm that aims to improve the performance and scalability of blockchains. This allows Cosmos to process more transactions per second than some traditional blockchains.

Governance is another essential pillar of Cosmos. The platform proposes a decentralized governance model where Atom token holders can participate in important decisions regarding the network's evolution. This promotes democracy and inclusivity within the Cosmos community.

The Cosmos network was officially launched in 2019 with the release of its main network called the Cosmos Hub. Since then, many other blockchains have joined the Cosmos ecosystem, each bringing its own value and contributing to the network's diversity.

Cosmos' native token, Atom, plays a central role in the ecosystem's operation. It is used for network security, participation in governance, and also serves as a means of exchange between different connected blockchains.

Cosmos has attracted attention due to its ambitious vision of creating an internet of blockchains, where different blockchains can interact seamlessly. This innovative approach has sparked interest from developers, businesses, and the crypto community at large. Cosmos has emerged as a major force in the cryptocurrency ecosystem, offering a versatile platform for the development of interconnected blockchains.

- ❖ **Solana** is a blockchain project that emerged in 2020 as a platform designed to offer exceptional scalability and transaction processing speed. Founded by Anatoly Yakovenko, Solana aims to address the scalability challenges facing many blockchains by providing a fast, secure, and decentralized infrastructure.

The core of Solana's technology relies on an innovative consensus mechanism called Proof of History (PoH), which chronologically organizes transactions before they are added to the blockchain. This significantly improves network efficiency and speed by reducing the time needed to reach consensus.

Solana also uses the Proof of Stake (PoS) consensus mechanism to validate blocks, allowing SOL token holders (Solana's native cryptocurrency) to participate in the consensus process based on their financial stake. This approach contributes to the security and decentralization of the network.

The Solana platform has attracted attention due to its exceptional performance, capable of handling a large number of transactions per second (TPS) at very low costs. This makes it an attractive option for decentralized applications (dApps) and DeFi (Decentralized Finance) projects that require high scalability.

Additionally, Solana offers a comprehensive development ecosystem with tools and resources for developers, making it easy to create decentralized applications on the Solana blockchain. Projects such as Serum, a decentralized trading platform built on Solana, demonstrate the diversity of possible applications on this blockchain.

Solana's development team continues to innovate, working on updates to further improve performance, security, and user experience. The growing

Solana community also contributes to its dynamic ecosystem, making it one of the emerging forces in the cryptocurrency universe.

These examples represent just a small selection of the many Altcoins available on the market. Each Altcoin offers specific features aimed at addressing particular challenges or providing new functionalities to users. By exploring the key characteristics of these Altcoins, investors and cryptocurrency enthusiasts can better understand the opportunities and differences offered by each project.

C. Classification of Cryptocurrencies

In the modern era of digital finance, cryptocurrencies have emerged as revolutionary assets, redefining how we perceive value, transactions, and the underlying technology. As the traditional world of financial markets continues to evolve, two online platforms have distinguished themselves as guiding beacons within the complex ecosystem of cryptocurrencies: CoinMarketCap and CoinGecko. These two websites are more than just sources of information; they have become indispensable references for investors, enthusiasts, and the curious looking to navigate the ever-changing world of cryptocurrencies.

CoinMarketCap quickly established itself as one of the most influential and reliable websites for tracking and analyzing thousands of cryptocurrencies available on the market. Offering a comprehensive overview of market data such as real-time prices, trading volumes, and market capitalizations, CoinMarketCap has become the starting point for those seeking to assess the performance and relevance of a particular cryptocurrency. Over the years, the platform has adapted to the changing needs of the crypto community by adding new features and expanding its scope to provide in-depth education on emerging projects and trends.

On the other hand, CoinGecko has brought a unique perspective to the cryptocurrency ecosystem by focusing on broader metrics to evaluate the value and viability of a project. In addition to classic market data, CoinGecko incorporates factors such as liquidity, community, technology, and the reliability of the team behind each cryptocurrency. This more nuanced approach offers users a more comprehensive and multidimensional view, helping them better understand the complex nuances of each project.

I will explain in detail the unique roles played by CoinMarketCap and CoinGecko in the constantly evolving crypto landscape. From how these platforms have shaped investment decisions to their impact on innovation within blockchain and cryptocurrencies, we will delve into the depths of these indispensable online resources, which continue to illuminate the path for enthusiasts of the cryptographic revolution.

First, here is an overview of the content of the CoinMarketCap website.

https://coinmarketcap.com

A – Introduction to CoinMarketCap

CoinMarketCap (CMC) is a leading platform that plays a central role in the ever-evolving world of cryptocurrencies. Founded in 2013 by Brandon Chez, CMC has risen to the top as a one-stop-shop for market data, analysis, and information regarding a wide range of cryptocurrencies and tokens. This platform provides users with a panoramic view of market performance, allowing them to track price fluctuations, trading volumes, and market capitalizations of thousands of digital assets. More than just a platform, CoinMarketCap has become a pillar of the crypto ecosystem, providing investors, traders, researchers, and the curious with essential tools to navigate this ever-changing financial landscape.

B - Market Data

At the heart of CoinMarketCap are market data that provide an in-depth and real-time overview of the cryptocurrency universe. Each cryptocurrency is meticulously documented with vital information such as current prices, trading volumes, and market capitalizations, providing users with a detailed view of market dynamics. This data enables investors and traders to make informed decisions, spot emerging trends, and identify potential trading opportunities within this often volatile environment.

C - Ranking

The ranking of cryptocurrencies by market capitalization is one of the most recognizable features of CoinMarketCap. This classification allows users to quickly assess the relative size of each cryptocurrency compared to others. Projects are ranked based on the total value of their circulating tokens, providing insight into the most significant and influential assets in the market. This dynamic hierarchy helps investors consider not only the individual prices of cryptocurrencies but also their overall importance within the ecosystem.

D - Cryptocurrency Details

Each dedicated page for a cryptocurrency on CoinMarketCap offers a wealth of information that goes beyond simple market data. Project details, information about the founding team, underlying technology, token distribution, and links to official websites allow users to deepen their knowledge of each cryptocurrency. This information is crucial for investors seeking to understand the fundamentals of a particular project, as well as for the curious looking to learn more about the disruptive technologies underlying these digital assets.

E - Historical Evolution

CoinMarketCap offers detailed historical charts that go back in time to display the evolution of prices and trading volumes of a cryptocurrency. These charts can be adjusted to display specific time intervals, ranging from minutes to years, allowing users to identify short-term and long-term trends. This feature is valuable for understanding how prices have evolved in the past and for analyzing market cycles that influence the current performance of cryptocurrencies.

F - Advanced Features

In addition to basic data, CoinMarketCap offers a multitude of advanced features to meet the diverse needs of users. Custom price alerts help investors closely monitor market movements by alerting them when prices reach predefined levels. Watchlists allow users to select and track their favorite cryptocurrencies, facilitating more focused portfolio management. Currency conversion calculators help estimate the value of cryptocurrencies in different fiat currencies, facilitating international comparisons and informed investment decisions.

G - Correlation Graph

An intriguing feature of CoinMarketCap is the correlation graph, which shows how different cryptocurrencies interact and evolve in tandem in the markets. This visual graph can help investors identify similar behavior patterns among different cryptocurrencies, which can have significant implications for diversification and investment strategies.

H - Application Programming Interface (API)

CoinMarketCap provides an Application Programming Interface (API) to allow developers to access real-time market data and integrate it into their custom applications and tools. This API has opened the door to a multitude of third-party applications that use CMC data to power custom dashboards, advanced analytics, and automated trading tools.

I - Educational Information

CoinMarketCap is not limited to market data alone; it is also committed to educating users about the fundamental principles of cryptocurrencies and blockchain technology. Through educational articles, guides, and tutorials, CoinMarketCap helps users understand key concepts such as blockchain, proof of work, proof of stake, digital wallets, and much more. This educational approach reinforces CMC's goal of fostering adoption and understanding of cryptocurrencies beyond simple market data.

J - Non-Fungible Tokens (NFTs)

In the wake of the rise of non-fungible tokens (NFTs), CoinMarketCap has expanded its scope to include this category of unique digital assets.

NFT pages provide information about creative projects, marketplace platforms, and auctions. This expansion reflects the ongoing evolution of the cryptocurrency ecosystem and CoinMarketCap's ability to stay up-to-date with the latest trends.

K - Rewards

CoinMarketCap has introduced "Rewards" to celebrate outstanding achievements in the field of cryptocurrencies. These rewards aim to highlight projects, individuals, and organizations that have made significant contributions to the adoption, innovation, and awareness of cryptocurrencies. The rewards underscore the importance of collaboration and progress within the crypto ecosystem.

L - Watchlist

CoinMarketCap's watchlist feature allows users to customize their experience by closely monitoring the performance of their favorite cryptocurrencies. By adding assets to their watchlist, investors can track real-time price changes, trading volumes, and other key indicators that matter most to them.

M - Liquidity Metrics

CoinMarketCap has introduced liquidity metrics to provide a more comprehensive perspective on how easily an asset can be bought or sold without significantly disrupting prices. These metrics help traders assess market efficiency for different cryptocurrencies, which is crucial for making informed decisions.

N - News and Updates

In addition to serving as a reference for market data, CoinMarketCap also serves as a source of news and updates for events, announcements, and major developments in the world of cryptocurrencies. Users can access the latest news and relevant analysis to stay informed about key trends and developments.

O - Conversion Tools

CoinMarketCap offers currency conversion tools that allow users to calculate the value of a cryptocurrency in different fiat currencies. These tools are useful for international users who wish to evaluate the value of their assets in their local currencies.

P - Virtual Portfolio While

CoinMarketCap does not offer an integrated wallet, users can create their own virtual portfolio by entering the quantities held of each cryptocurrency. This allows them to track the total value of their portfolio over time. While less advanced than an external wallet, this provides users with a simple way to monitor their investments.

The CMC app is available to view your portfolio on your phone.

Q - Exchange Quality

A unique feature of CoinMarketCap is the evaluation of exchange quality. By providing information on liquidity, trading volumes, and other parameters, CoinMarketCap helps users assess the reliability and integrity of listed exchange platforms. This transparency enhances users' confidence in choosing exchanges on which to trade.

R - Social Media and Community

Dedicated pages for each cryptocurrency on CoinMarketCap also include links to social media accounts and online communities associated with each project. This allows users to follow news, discussions, and developments in real-time, as well as engage with teams and other community members.

S - Global Statistics

CoinMarketCap also provides global statistics that offer an overview of the entire cryptocurrency market. This includes the total number of listed cryptocurrencies, total market capitalization, daily trading volume, and other aggregates that illustrate the scale and dynamics of the crypto ecosystem.

T - Trends

CoinMarketCap's trend service allows users to track the latest market developments. Trends reveal the top-performing cryptocurrencies, emerging news, projects to watch, and significant changes in market capitalization rankings. This helps users stay informed about important developments and emerging opportunities.

CoinMarketCap is much more than just a market data platform; it is an invaluable resource that gives users comprehensive access to the global cryptocurrency ecosystem. From real-time market data to detailed project information, from advanced features to news and analysis, CoinMarketCap continues to play an essential role in expanding, understanding, and adopting cryptocurrencies on a global scale.

Next is an overview of the content of the CoinGecko website.

https://www.coingecko.com

A. Introduction to CoinGecko

CoinGecko is a comprehensive platform that holds a central position in the cryptocurrency ecosystem by providing a multitude of essential information and tools. Founded in 2014 by TM Lee and Bobby Ong, CoinGecko quickly established itself as an indispensable resource for cryptocurrency enthusiasts, investors, and industry experts. The platform strives to deliver quality data, in-depth analysis, and innovative features to enable users to make informed decisions in a constantly evolving financial space.

B. Market Data

CoinGecko offers a rich source of market data for thousands of cryptocurrencies and tokens. Users can access real-time information on prices, trading volumes, market capitalizations, exchange rates, and much more. This data provides a comprehensive overview of digital asset performance, allowing investors and traders to track trends and identify market opportunities.

C. Ranking

Cryptocurrencies on CoinGecko are ranked based on a unique metric called "Gecko Rank." This metric takes into account factors such as liquidity, development activity, community, market capitalization, and other indicators. Ranking based on "Gecko Rank" offers a more holistic perspective on the value and relevance of projects compared to other ranking platforms.

D. Cryptocurrency Details

Dedicated pages for cryptocurrencies on CoinGecko provide in-depth information about each project. In addition to market data, users can explore details such as the development team, key features, networks on which the cryptocurrency operates, links to websites and social media accounts, as well as other crucial information to understand the nature and purpose of a project.

E. Historical Evolution

CoinGecko offers historical price and trading volume charts for each cryptocurrency. These charts allow users to analyze past performance and market trends over different time periods. This feature is essential for evaluating historical volatility and making informed decisions based on past market behavior.

F. Advanced Features

In addition to market data, CoinGecko offers advanced features such as custom price alerts, virtual portfolios, news notifications, and customized watchlists. Price alerts help users stay informed when prices reach specific thresholds. Virtual portfolios allow users to track their investments over time. News notifications keep users informed about industry developments. Custom watchlists allow users to keep an eye on assets that matter most to them.

G. Correlation Graph

CoinGecko's correlation graph allows users to visualize relationships between different cryptocurrencies in terms of market performance. This can help identify common market trends and synchronized movements among digital assets, providing insight into market behavior.

H. Application Programming Interface (API)

CoinGecko also offers an API that allows developers to access market data and cryptocurrency information to integrate into their own applications and tools. This API facilitates the creation of custom applications, advanced analytical tools, and innovative solutions based on CoinGecko data.

I. Educational Information

CoinGecko not only provides market data but also aims to educate users about key concepts and trends in the cryptocurrency space. The platform offers educational articles, guides, in-depth analysis, and explanations about underlying technologies, protocols, and industry developments. This educational approach aims to enhance users' understanding and engagement in the crypto ecosystem.

J. Non-Fungible Tokens (NFTs)

CoinGecko has also expanded its scope to include non-fungible tokens (NFTs). Dedicated pages for NFTs provide information about projects, creators, and NFT platforms, allowing users to track developments in this booming field.

K. Rewards

CoinGecko has introduced "Rewards" as a way to recognize and celebrate key players in the cryptocurrency ecosystem. These rewards aim to highlight projects, individuals, and companies that have made significant contributions to the industry. Rewards underscore the importance of innovation, collaboration, and excellence within the crypto community.

L. Watchlist

CoinGecko's customized watchlist allows users to select and monitor their favorite cryptocurrencies. This feature enables targeted performance tracking, facilitating digital asset management and monitoring of projects that matter most to users.

M. Liquidity Metrics

CoinGecko incorporates liquidity metrics that provide information on the ease of trading a cryptocurrency across different exchanges. This helps users assess the availability and liquidity of digital assets in the market.

N. News and Updates

In addition to market data, CoinGecko provides real-time news and updates on the cryptocurrency industry. This allows users to stay informed about major events, project announcements, technological developments, and emerging trends.

O. Conversion Tools

CoinGecko offers currency conversion tools to assess the value of cryptocurrencies in different fiat currencies. These tools facilitate international comparisons and help users understand the value of their investments in their local currency.

P. Virtual Portfolio

While CoinGecko does not offer an integrated wallet, users can utilize the virtual portfolio feature to track and manage their investments. They can enter quantities held of each cryptocurrency and track the total value of their portfolio over time.

Q. Exchange Quality

CoinGecko provides information on the quality of listed exchanges, including data on liquidity, trading volumes, price spreads, and other indicators. This helps users choose trading platforms that offer the best conditions and most reliable experiences.

R. Social Media and Community

Dedicated pages for cryptocurrencies on CoinGecko include links to social media accounts and online communities associated with each project. This allows users to follow discussions, news, and developments related to each cryptocurrency.

S. Global Statistics

CoinGecko offers global statistics on the entire cryptocurrency market, including the total number of cryptocurrencies, total market capitalization, daily trading volume, and other aggregated data. These statistics provide users with insight into the scale and dynamics of the market.

T. Trends

CoinGecko's trend section highlights top-performing cryptocurrencies, projects to watch, and major industry developments. This allows users to stay informed about recent developments and emerging opportunities in the world of cryptocurrencies.

CoinGecko is an invaluable resource that goes beyond market data, offering users detailed information, in-depth analysis, and advanced features to navigate the cryptocurrency ecosystem. From real-time market data to project information, user-friendly features, and relevant news, CoinGecko serves as an essential guide for industry players, whether they are novices or experienced.

Main differences

While they share similarities, they also present significant differences. Here are the main differences between CoinMarketCap and CoinGecko :

1. **Market Data :**

Both platforms provide market data such as prices, trading volumes, and market capitalizations. However, values may vary slightly due to differences in data sources and calculation methods.

2. **Advanced Features :**

CoinMarketCap offers features such as price alerts, customized watchlists, historical charts, and detailed cryptocurrency information. CoinGecko offers similar features, as well as currency conversion tools, virtual portfolios, news notifications, and liquidity metrics.

3. **In-Depth Analysis :**

CoinGecko is often recognized for providing more in-depth analysis of projects, including details about teams, technical features, news, and upcoming developments. CoinMarketCap focuses more on market data and provides basic information about projects.

4. **API and Integrations :**

Both platforms offer APIs (Application Programming Interfaces) to allow developers to access market data and cryptocurrency information.

5. **User Experience :**

CoinGecko is often considered to have a more user-friendly interface, with clear information presentation and intuitive navigation. CoinMarketCap has undergone design changes over time, but some past criticisms have focused on the complexity of navigation.

6. Educational Content :

CoinGecko also provides educational content, articles, and guides to help users better understand the world of cryptocurrencies and blockchain.

7. Evolution and Updates :

CoinGecko has rapidly evolved to include features such as non-fungible tokens (NFTs) and rewards. CoinMarketCap has also expanded its scope to track industry developments, including NFTs.

8. Availability of Cryptocurrencies :

New low-cap cryptocurrencies are first listed on CoinGecko, and then on CoinMarketCap.

In summary, while CoinMarketCap and CoinGecko share the goal of providing information about cryptocurrencies, their ranking methods, features, and editorial approaches differ. Users can choose the platform that best meets their needs for information, tools, and analysis to navigate the complex world of cryptocurrencies.

D. Specific Uses of Altcoins

Altcoins, or "Alternative Altcoins," refer to all cryptocurrencies other than Bitcoin, which is often considered the first and most well-known of them. Over the years, the cryptocurrency ecosystem has grown significantly, giving rise to thousands of Altcoins, each with specific characteristics and objectives. These Altcoins have found various uses in the world of decentralized finance, blockchain technology, and decentralized applications.

First and foremost, Altcoins play a crucial role in diversifying investment portfolios. While Bitcoin has gained massive popularity as a store of value, some Altcoins have proven to be innovative projects with concrete use cases. Investors seek to diversify their cryptocurrency holdings by allocating some of their funds to promising Altcoins, hoping for potentially higher long-term returns.

Secondly, some Altcoins are designed to address specific problems that are not fully addressed by Bitcoin or other traditional technologies. For example, Ethereum, one of the first major Altcoins, introduced smart contracts, which allow for the automatic execution of programmed conditions, paving the way for decentralized applications, DeFi (Decentralized Finance) protocols, and asset tokenization.

Altcoins are also used as utility or governance tokens for platforms and decentralized applications. These tokens can be used to access certain services, pay transaction fees, participate in governance votes, or be rewarded for participating in specific networks.

Some Altcoins focus on anonymity and privacy, offering alternatives to public blockchain transactions. These privacy-focused cryptocurrencies have found use in areas where privacy is crucial, such as e-commerce, cross-border fund transfers, or confidential business operations.

Additionally, some Altcoins target specific industries such as healthcare, energy, logistics, or gaming. They aim to optimize processes and solve specific problems encountered in these areas using blockchain technology.

Finally, Altcoins often serve as means of exchange for purchasing goods and services, thereby expanding the acceptance of cryptocurrencies in daily commerce.

It is important to note that the Altcoin market is highly dynamic, and many projects emerge and disappear rapidly. Some Altcoins experience dramatic price increases, while others may be subject to volatility or even fraud. Therefore, users must exercise caution and due diligence when choosing to use Altcoins, seeking out well-established projects with a strong team, a clear roadmap, and robust technology.

E. Comparison with Bitcoin and Other Major Cryptocurrencies

Cryptocurrencies Bitcoin, as the first cryptocurrency ever created, paved the way for the emergence of a decentralized financial ecosystem and played a crucial role in introducing the concept of blockchain to the world. However, there are many other major cryptocurrencies, often referred to as Altcoins, that have developed with specific features and objectives and now compete with Bitcoin in the cryptocurrency market.

One of the main differences between Bitcoin and Altcoins lies in their underlying technologies and objectives. Bitcoin is primarily designed as a digital store of value and is often compared to digital gold. It aims to provide a form of digital money that is resistant to inflation and censorship, with a total supply limited to 21 million bitcoins. In contrast, many Altcoins have been developed to address specific problems and introduce advanced features. For example, Ethereum brought smart contracts and paved the way for decentralized applications and DeFi protocols. Other Altcoins focus on anonymity, privacy, or target specific industries such as healthcare, energy, or gaming. Vitalik Buterin, co-founder of Ethereum, is a key figure in the smart contracts field and has contributed to shaping the evolution of this technology.

Another aspect of the comparison between Bitcoin and Altcoins concerns security and decentralization. Bitcoin is often praised for its enhanced security as a decentralized and censorship-resistant network, thanks to its Proof of Work consensus algorithm. However, some Altcoins have opted for different approaches, such as Proof of Stake or other variants, to achieve decentralized consensus while improving network energy efficiency.

Price volatility is also an important factor when comparing Bitcoin and Altcoins. Historically, Bitcoin has been subject to significant price fluctuations but is often considered less volatile than some less-established and lower-cap Altcoins. Altcoins may experience dramatic price increases, but they are also prone to brutal corrections. This can be both an opportunity and a risk for investors.

Regarding adoption and awareness, Bitcoin has dominated the cryptocurrency market since its creation and is generally better known to the general public compared to most Altcoins. However, some Altcoins have gained popularity and adoption in specific areas. For example, Ripple (XRP) has attracted attention from the banking sector for its cross-border payment solutions, while Litecoin (LTC) is often seen as a faster and cheaper alternative to Bitcoin for transactions.

Finally, regulation and government policies can also play a role in the comparison between Bitcoin and Altcoins. Some countries have adopted specific laws regarding cryptocurrencies, which may influence their adoption and use in certain jurisdictions.

Overall, the comparison between Bitcoin and other major cryptocurrencies is complex and depends on the specific needs of each user. While Bitcoin continues to be a major digital asset and store of value, Altcoins offer a variety of options to address specific use cases and may present unique investment opportunities. It is essential to understand the characteristics, objectives, and risks associated with each cryptocurrency before making informed investment decisions in this constantly evolving universe.

F. Security of Bitcoin and Cryptocurrencies

The security of Bitcoin relies on several key elements, including private keys, wallets, and the security protocol. Here is an explanation of each of these elements :

- **Private Key :** A private key is a randomly generated and cryptographically secure string of characters. It is essential for accessing and controlling a user's bitcoins. The private key must be kept secret because anyone who possesses it can access the associated funds. Private keys are used to sign transactions, thereby proving ownership of the bitcoins.

- **Wallets :** A Bitcoin wallet is software or a physical device that stores private keys and allows users to manage their bitcoins. There are several types of wallets, such as software wallets (applications for computers or mobile devices), hardware wallets (dedicated physical devices), and paper wallets (private keys printed on paper). Wallets provide a user-friendly interface for sending, receiving, and storing bitcoins.

Here are some examples of commonly used storage mediums for private keys:

- **Paper :** A private key can be printed on paper in the form of a QR code or text. This can be accomplished using an online paper wallet generator or wallet software that supports this feature.

- **Hardware Wallet :** Popular hardware wallets such as Ledger Nano S, Trezor, and KeepKey are examples of secure physical devices designed to store private keys. They use dedicated security elements to protect private keys from unauthorized access.

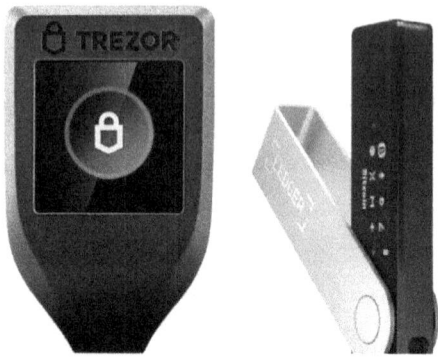

➢ **Software Wallet :** Wallet software such as Metamask, Trustwallet, Electrum, Exodus, Bitcoin Core, and MyEtherWallet allow users to store private keys on their computer, smartphone, or tablet. Private keys are typically stored in encrypted files on the device.

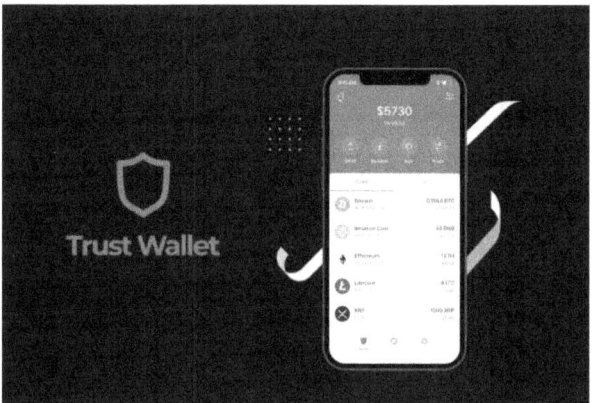

➢ **Online Wallet :** Online wallet platforms like Coinbase, Kraken, and Binance offer the option to store private keys on their servers. However, it is important to note that security depends on the platform and the trust you place in their security management. An example illustrating user vulnerability can be seen in the closure of the FTX platform, where users unfortunately lost all the funds they had deposited on that platform.

> **Multisignature Wallet :** A multisignature wallet is a type of wallet that requires multiple signatures to authorize a transaction. Private keys are distributed among multiple parties, adding an extra layer of security. Wallets such as Copay, BitGo, and Electrum offer this feature.

Vitalik Buterin, the co-founder of Ethereum, is often cited as a proponent of the multisignature wallet concept. Although he is not directly associated with a specific multisignature wallet, he has advocated for the use of this feature to enhance the security of cryptocurrency funds.

A concrete example of a project related to Vitalik Buterin and using a multisignature wallet is the Gnosis project.

Gnosis is an Ethereum-based platform that offers market prediction and decentralized governance services. Gnosis has developed a multisignature wallet called "Gnosis Safe." This wallet allows users to store their private keys and perform secure transactions using multiple signatures to authorize fund movements.

The Gnosis Safe wallet offers more secure fund management by allowing users to define multiple signers for the same wallet address. This means that to execute a transaction, it is necessary to obtain approval from a certain number of pre-defined signers. This feature adds an extra layer of security because even if one signer is compromised, the funds remain secure as long as the other signers do not approve the transaction.

> **Security Protocol :** The Bitcoin protocol itself is designed to offer a high level of security. It relies on cryptography technology to ensure the confidentiality, integrity, and security of transactions. Transactions are verified and recorded on the blockchain in a transparent and secure manner. The Bitcoin network also uses consensus mechanisms, such as proof of work, to prevent malicious attacks and ensure network security:

"Not Your Keys, Not Your Coins" is a fundamental principle in the cryptocurrency world. This phrase highlights the importance of owning and controlling your private keys to ensure the security of your digital funds.

When you entrust your private keys to third parties, such as exchange platforms or online wallets, you lose direct control of your assets. This exposes you to risks such as hacks, platform closures, or management errors. History has shown that many users have lost their funds due to the failure of these trusted third parties. (as we have just seen previously).

The private key is the only way to prove ownership and access your cryptocurrencies. By securely storing it, for example, in a hardware wallet or using a safephrase to back up your keys, you maintain total control over your digital assets.

The principle "Not Your Keys, Not Your Coins" reminds users of the importance of individual responsibility in managing their cryptocurrencies. It encourages users to take appropriate security measures to protect their private keys and to avoid excessive reliance on trusted third parties.

By adopting a security-focused approach and mastering your private keys, you ensure the protection of your funds and contribute to the decentralized and autonomous vision underlying cryptocurrencies. Be proactive, informed, and aware of the risks associated with managing private keys, as it is your responsibility to ensure the security of your digital assets in this constantly evolving ecosystem.

G. Growth Potential

The growth potential of cryptocurrencies has been a major topic of interest since the emergence of Bitcoin in 2009. This class of digital assets has attracted the attention of many well-known figures from the finance and technology sectors who have expressed their views on their future.

Among the notable figures who have expressed optimism about the growth potential of cryptocurrencies is Michael Saylor, CEO of MicroStrategy, who has become a staunch advocate of Bitcoin as a store of value. Saylor converted a significant portion of his company's cash reserves into Bitcoin, viewing the cryptocurrency as a hedge against inflation and a long-term investment strategy.

Billionaire Elon Musk, founder of Tesla and SpaceX, is also an influential figure in the world of cryptocurrencies. While he has expressed both support and concerns about cryptocurrencies, his tweets and statements have often had a significant impact on the prices of digital assets, especially Bitcoin and Dogecoin.

Jack Dorsey, CEO of Twitter and founder of Square, has invested in Bitcoin and believes in its long-term potential.

Notable figures from the traditional financial industry have also shown interest in cryptocurrencies. Billionaire Paul Tudor Jones, a renowned investor and hedge fund manager, announced that he had invested in

Bitcoin as a hedge against inflation and compared its growth potential to that of gold in the 1970s.

Additionally, brothers Tyler and Cameron Winklevoss, known for their role in creating Facebook, are now major players in the cryptocurrency industry. They founded the cryptocurrency exchange platform Gemini and are strong advocates of Bitcoin as a store of value and the cryptocurrency ecosystem as a whole.

The aforementioned individuals are just a sampling of influential individuals who have helped draw attention to the growth potential of cryptocurrencies. Their involvement and support have contributed to increased acceptance of digital assets among the general public, as well as in financial and technological circles.

The growth potential of cryptocurrencies rests on several key factors, including increasing adoption by businesses and financial institutions, recognition by governments and regulators, improvements in infrastructure and underlying technology, as well as growing demand for decentralized and inclusive financial solutions.

While the cryptocurrency market is subject to considerable volatility and regulatory challenges, many experts believe that the innovation and continued evolution of this ecosystem could offer significant long-term growth potential.

IV. Smart Investment: Dollar-Cost Averaging in Cryptocurrencies

A. Principle of DCA and Why It's Useful for Cryptocurrency Investment

In the world of investing, timing the market can be a tricky endeavor. Trying to predict the exact moment when an asset's price will reach its peak or bottom can be a daunting task, often leading to impulsive decisions driven by emotions rather than sound financial reasoning. This is where Dollar-Cost Averaging (DCA) emerges as a savior for investors seeking a more structured and disciplined approach.

DCA, a widely-recognized investment strategy, involves investing a fixed amount of money in a particular asset at regular intervals, regardless of its current market price. This systematic approach aims to smooth out the average cost per unit of the asset over time, taking advantage of price fluctuations to maximize the number of units acquired during periods of low prices and minimizing the number purchased when prices are high.

By adopting a DCA strategy, investors can effectively avoid the pitfalls of emotional investing, which often lead to buying assets at inflated prices during market rallies and selling them at rock-bottom prices during downturns. Instead, DCA instills a sense of discipline, encouraging investors to stay invested consistently, regardless of market conditions.

This strategy is particularly beneficial in the realm of cryptocurrency investments, where market volatility and unpredictable price movements are common. By investing regularly using DCA, investors can spread out their purchases over time, reducing the overall risk associated with investing in a single instance. For instance, by investing a fixed amount in a cryptocurrency each month, the investor's average cost per unit will be determined by the fluctuating market prices throughout the investment period. This means that during periods of price dips, the investor will be able to acquire more tokens for the same amount of money, while during periods of price surges, they will purchase fewer tokens. This approach effectively maximizes investment returns while minimizing the risks associated with lump-sum investments.

In essence, Dollar-Cost Averaging serves as a powerful tool for investors navigating the often unpredictable waters of volatile markets like cryptocurrencies. By embracing DCA, investors can instill discipline, minimize emotional decision-making, and potentially enhance their long-term investment returns. While market fluctuations may persist, DCA provides a sound strategy for weathering the storms and emerging as informed and resilient investors.

Investors can thus avoid falling into the trap of impulsive and emotional investment, which can lead them to buy financial assets at high prices during periods of strong growth or sell at low prices during periods of steep decline.

Dollar Cost Averaging (DCA) is particularly useful in the context of cryptocurrency investment, which is a volatile market often difficult to predict. By investing regularly and using DCA, investors can minimize investment risks by spreading their purchases over a given period rather than investing all at once. For example, by investing a fixed amount each month in a cryptocurrency, the investor will benefit from an average acquisition cost, calculated by taking into account the fluctuating market prices over the investment period. Thus, if the cryptocurrency price drops, the investor can buy more tokens for the same amount of money, while if it increases, they will buy fewer. This strategy maximizes investment returns by minimizing the risks of loss associated with investing all at once.

DCA can also help investors guard against psychological pitfalls such as fear or greed, which can lead to impulsive or emotional decisions. By investing regularly, investors focus on the overall performance of their investment rather than short-term market fluctuations.

DCA is a very useful investment strategy for cryptocurrency investors, as it helps reduce risks associated with market volatility and maximize long-term gains. By implementing an effective DCA plan, investors can confidently invest in cryptocurrencies while minimizing investment-related risks.

B. How to Implement an Effective DCA Plan

To implement DCA in cryptocurrencies, several steps should be followed. Here's an example of setting up a DCA plan for Bitcoin and Ethereum :

- **Choose a reliable exchange platform :** First, choose a reliable exchange platform that allows buying and selling cryptocurrencies. There are many options available, such as Coinbase, Kraken, or Binance.

- **Define a budget and investment frequency :** Next, define a monthly or weekly budget for investing in cryptocurrencies, as well as an investment frequency (e.g., monthly or weekly). This budget and frequency should be adapted to the investor's financial capabilities.

- **Purchase regularly :** At each investment period, the investor buys the same amount of Bitcoin or Ethereum, regardless of the cryptocurrency's price at that time. For example, if the investor decides to invest 100 euros per month in Bitcoin, they will buy 100 euros worth of Bitcoin each month, regardless of whether the price has increased or decreased since the previous month.

- **Periodically reassess the DCA :** It's essential to periodically reassess the DCA plan based on market developments and the investor's financial capabilities. If the market is highly volatile and price fluctuations are significant, adjusting the budget and investment frequency to better adapt to the market may be wise.

Taking a concrete example, suppose you want to invest in Bitcoin and Ethereum with a monthly budget of 200 euros. You decide to allocate this budget as follows :

- 100 euros per month in Bitcoin
- 100 euros per month in Ethereum

Every month, you buy 100 euros worth of Bitcoin and 100 euros worth of

Ethereum, regardless of their current prices. Then, you reassess your DCA plan quarterly to adjust your budget and investment frequency based on market evolution.

By implementing DCA, you can invest regularly in cryptocurrencies while minimizing risks associated with market volatility.

C. Concrete Examples and Simulations to Illustrate Potential Gains with DCA

A concrete example of DCA's effectiveness comes from the renowned American economist Benjamin Graham. In his book "The Intelligent Investor," Graham recommends using a DCA strategy for stock investment. He explains that this strategy allows buying shares at different prices, thus reducing the risk of losing money if the market turns.

To illustrate DCA's effectiveness, let's consider Investor A and Investor B. Investor A invests 1000 euros in a stock in one go, while Investor B invests 100 euros per month in the same stock, following a DCA strategy.

Suppose the stock is priced at 10 euros at the beginning of the year. During the first six months of the year, the stock rises to 15 euros and then falls back to 10 euros at the end of the year.

Here are the results for each investor :

Investor A invested 1000 euros at the beginning of the year and ended the year with a loss of 500 euros (1000 euros - 500 euros).

Investor B invested 600 euros (100 euros per month for six months) and ended the year with a gain of 25 euros ((500 euros of shares bought at 10 euros) + (100 euros of shares bought at 15 euros) - (600 euros invested in total)).

In this example, Investor B benefited from the DCA strategy by reducing their risk and achieving a better return than Investor A.

Many economists and financial experts also recommend using DCA, including Warren Buffett. He stated in an interview that "for most people, the best way to invest in stocks is to invest regularly over time. [...] Buying one stock at a time can be a costly mistake."

Therefore, DCA helps limit risks associated with market volatility by purchasing assets at regular intervals, which can generate long-term gains.

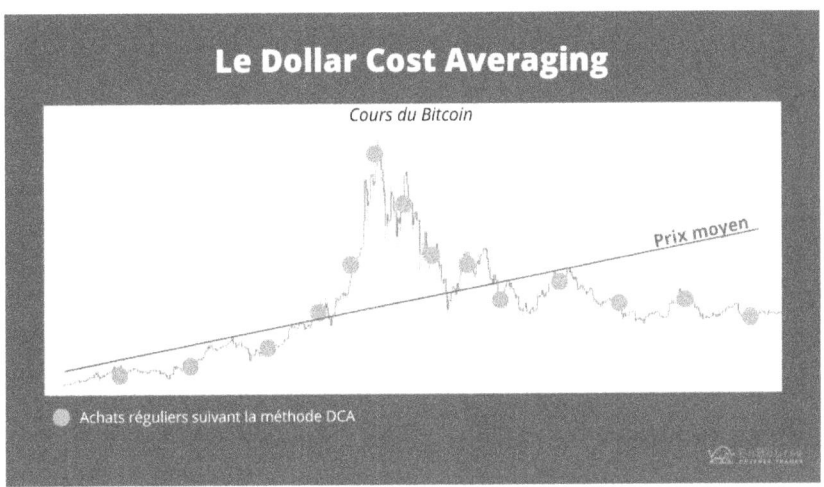

Tailoring Crypto Portfolios to Diverse Investment Styles : Navigating the Risk-Reward Spectrum

The realm of cryptocurrency investments presents a diverse landscape of opportunities, each carrying its own set of potential rewards and inherent risks. As an investor, understanding your risk tolerance, financial goals, and investment preferences is paramount to crafting a portfolio that aligns with your unique style and objectives.

Conservative Investors : Embracing Stability and Established Assets

For those prioritizing stability and familiarity, a conservative approach often involves focusing on well-established cryptocurrencies with a proven track record and a strong community backing. Bitcoin and Ethereum, the two leading cryptocurrencies by market capitalization, often form the cornerstone of conservative portfolios.

Balanced Investors : Diversifying Across Market Capitalizations

Balanced investors seek a blend of stability and growth potential by diversifying their portfolios across a wider range of cryptocurrencies. While still maintaining a core holding of established assets, they may also venture into the top 100 cryptocurrencies by market capitalization, exploring projects with promising use cases and innovation potential.

Risk-Tolerant Investors : Venturing into the Realm of High-Potential Altcoins

Risk-tolerant investors are drawn to the high-growth potential of smaller, less established cryptocurrencies, often referred to as altcoins. While these investments carry a higher degree of risk, they also offer the possibility of explosive returns. However, it's essential to exercise caution, conduct thorough research, and diversify across multiple altcoins to mitigate risks.

Key Considerations for Building Your Crypto Portfolio

- **Risk Tolerance :** Assess your comfort level with potential losses and tailor your investment strategy accordingly.

- **Financial Goals :** Define your investment objectives, whether it's long-term wealth accumulation or short-term profit-taking.

- **Investment Preferences :** Choose between established cryptocurrencies, promising altcoins, or a combination of both.

- **Diversification :** Spread your investments across different assets to reduce risk and increase the likelihood of success.

- **Research :** Conduct in-depth research on each cryptocurrency, evaluating its fundamentals, team, and market potential.

- **Emotional Control :** Avoid impulsive decisions driven by market hype or fear. Stick to your investment plan and make informed choices.

Remember, there is no one-size-fits-all approach to cryptocurrency investing. The key lies in understanding your own risk profile, financial goals, and investment preferences, and crafting a portfolio that aligns with your individual needs.

By carefully considering these factors, you can navigate the dynamic world of cryptocurrencies with confidence, building a portfolio that reflects your unique investment style and maximizes your chances of achieving your financial goals.

Cryptocurrency Investor Portfolios : Diverse Styles for Varied Goals

Cautious Investor: Safety and Classic Choices

The cautious investor prioritizes stability and recognition. Their portfolio consists of 50% Bitcoin, the flagship cryptocurrency, and 50% Ethereum, the leader in smart contracts. They prefer to walk on the safe side of the road, but with style!

Playful but Savvy Investor: A Touch of Risk to Spice Things Up

The playful investor, while remaining cautious, is not afraid to take a few calculated risks. Their portfolio consists of 30% Bitcoin, because you can't ignore the king of cryptocurrencies, 30% Ethereum, because they know there's magic in smart contracts, and they add a touch of whimsy by investing in a few cryptocurrencies from the top 100 of Coinmarketcap. After all, they like to have a few tricks up their sleeve to keep things interesting!

Daring Investor: On the Hunt for the Hidden Gem

The daring investor is not afraid to take risks and turns to small-cap cryptocurrencies, those hiding beyond the top 100 of Coinmarketcap. They are on the lookout for the hidden gem that could skyrocket them to the moon! However, they are also aware that they should not put all their eggs in one basket, or they could end up with a crypto omelet instead of a fortune. A little caution is always necessary, even for the most daring!

Remember :

- Humor is the spice of life, but investing should not be taken lightly.
- Always do your own research and make informed decisions.
- Cryptocurrency markets can be volatile, so keep your nerve and your sense of humor intact.

V. Taking Profits in a Bull Market

A. Why It's Important to Regularly Take Profits

Regular profit-taking in a bull market of cryptocurrencies is crucial for several reasons. Firstly, cryptocurrency volatility can be extremely high, meaning their value can fluctuate rapidly and unpredictably. Therefore, if you don't regularly take profits, you risk losing a significant portion of your gains if the market suddenly collapses.

Secondly, by regularly taking profits, you can also reduce your exposure to market risks. If you hold a large amount of cryptocurrencies and the market suddenly reverses, you could lose a significant portion of your capital in one go. By taking regular profits, you can reduce your risk exposure by selling some of your positions as the market rises.

Additionally, by regularly taking profits, you can also take advantage of short-term investment opportunities. If you see an interesting investment opportunity, you can sell some of your positions to realize profits and invest in that opportunity.

Finally, regularly taking profits can also help you achieve your long-term financial goals. By selling positions and realizing profits, you can reinvest these funds in other assets or use the gains to achieve other financial goals, such as buying a house or planning your retirement.

John Maynard Keynes, one of the most influential economists of the 20th century, often emphasized the importance of regularly taking profits in his writings. He notably stated, "It is rarely profitable to postpone taking profits. This does not reduce risk but rather increases the risk of greater loss."

Keynes also highlighted the importance of caution in investment management and encouraged investors to adopt a prudent and strategic approach to maximize their long-term returns. By regularly taking profits, investors can reduce their exposure to market risks and achieve consistent gains while preserving part of their capital for future investment opportunities.

In summary, Keynes advocated for a prudent and strategic approach to investment management, which includes regularly taking profits to reduce risks and maximize long-term returns.

Selling at the absolute peak and buying at the absolute bottom is extremely difficult, if not impossible. This reality is due to several factors :

- **Price volatility** : Cryptocurrency markets are known for their high volatility. Prices can rapidly rise (bull market) or fall (bear market) due to various factors such as supply and demand, economic news, regulation, etc. Predicting these movements precisely is extremely challenging.

- **Asymmetric information** : Market participants do not all have access to the same information simultaneously. Some institutional investors or large companies may have access to privileged information that is not available to the general public. This can make it difficult for small investors to seize opportunities at the right moment.

- **Market psychology** : Human emotions, such as fear and greed, play a significant role in financial markets. Investors can be influenced by panic during downturns or by euphoria during upturns, leading them to make irrational decisions.

➤ **Market manipulation :** Cryptocurrency markets can be subject to price manipulation by malicious actors. This can lead to artificial price movements that do not necessarily follow market fundamentals.

Due to these factors, attempting to sell at the peak or buy at the bottom is considered market timing, a very risky strategy that can lead to significant losses. Professional and experienced investors generally use risk management and diversification approaches to handle market fluctuations, rather than trying to perfectly time their transactions.

Investing in cryptocurrencies, like other financial assets, requires a cautious approach, based on thorough research, an understanding of risks, and clear investment objectives.

B. How to Set a Realistic Profit Target

Defining a realistic profit target to become a millionaire in the cryptocurrency market requires careful analysis of key market factors. This includes cryptocurrency price volatility, supply and demand, adoption and usage of cryptocurrencies, as well as competition with other financial assets.

The first step is to determine how much money you are willing to invest in cryptocurrencies. Then, you need to consider the period over which you want to achieve this goal. It's important to note that the shorter the period, the higher the risk, as cryptocurrency markets can be extremely volatile.

A commonly used strategy for defining a realistic profit target is to focus on a percentage gain rather than a specific amount. For example, if you want to become a millionaire by investing in cryptocurrencies, you could aim for a 1000% gain on your initial investment.

Next, you need to examine the past performance of the cryptocurrency market and current trends to assess whether this target is realistic. For example, if the cryptocurrency market has averaged a 200% annual growth rate in recent years, a 1000% gain over a 5-year period may seem achievable.

It's important to note that the cryptocurrency market is highly volatile and unpredictable, so guaranteeing results is difficult. You should also take into account transaction fees and tax implications when defining your profit target.

To define a realistic profit target to become a millionaire in the cryptocurrency market, you need to determine how much money you are willing to invest, the period over which you want to achieve this goal, and consider current trends and past performance of the market. You can then aim for a realistic percentage gain rather than a specific amount, while keeping in mind that cryptocurrency markets are volatile and unpredictable.

C. Strategies for Gradually Selling Cryptocurrencies

Having an exit strategy: Define profit and loss targets in advance to avoid losing money. Progressive selling of cryptocurrencies is a prudent strategy to manage risks and optimize profits. Here are some strategies for gradually selling your cryptocurrencies :

- ➢ **Define a profit target :** Before investing, determine a realistic profit target. Set a price level at which you would be satisfied to realize gains. When the price reaches this target, you can sell some of your cryptocurrencies to secure some profits.
- ➢ **Set a loss threshold :** Also, establish an acceptable loss threshold. If the cryptocurrency price declines and reaches this threshold, consider selling some of your assets to limit your losses. Having an exit plan in case of price declines is essential to preserve your capital.
- ➢ **Staggered sale:** Instead of selling a large quantity of cryptocurrencies all at once, consider staggered sales (reverse DCA). You can set different price levels to sell portions of your assets as the price increases. This allows you to benefit from potential additional gains if the price continues to rise.
- ➢ **Monitor market trends :** Keep a close eye on market trends. If the cryptocurrency price reaches historical highs or resistance levels, it may be wise to sell some of your assets to take profits. Similarly, if the market shows signs of turning downwards, you may want to reassess your strategy and reduce your exposure to cryptocurrencies.
- ➢ **Diversification :** Diversifying your cryptocurrency portfolio can also be a strategy to limit risks. By holding different cryptocurrencies, you can spread risks and benefit from growth opportunities in various projects.
- ➢ **Keep a portion of your investment long-term :** If you believe in

the long-term potential of certain cryptocurrencies, it may be wise to retain a portion of your investment for the long term. This allows you to benefit from potential long-term growth while realizing partial profits through gradual sales.

Remember that the cryptocurrency market is highly volatile and subject to significant fluctuations. Having a clear and well-defined exit strategy helps you make more rational decisions and avoid letting your emotions influence your investment choices.

Always remember one important thing : in the cryptocurrency market, for every person experiencing a loss, there is always someone else making a profit.

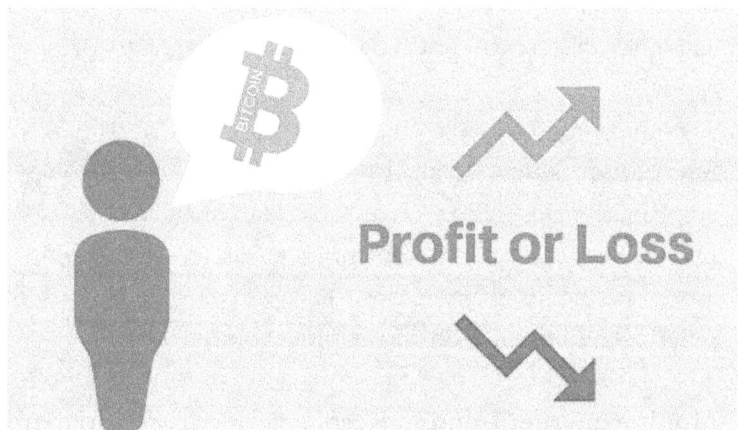

VI. Investing in Solid Projects and Diversifying Your Portfolio

A. How to Identify Solid Projects and Avoid Scams

Identifying solid cryptocurrency projects is an important step for investors. Here are some key elements to consider to avoid scams and identify quality projects:

- **Team and Transparency :** The quality of the development team is essential for a cryptocurrency project. It's important to research information about the development team, their backgrounds, experience, and transparency about their work. Transparent projects that clearly present the development team generally have more credibility.

- **Technology :** The underlying technology of the project should be clearly explained and understood. Projects with solid and innovative technology are more likely to succeed in the long term. It's also important to check the robustness of the protocol, blockchain security, and the existence of security audits.

- **Utility and Adoption :** Cryptocurrency projects must offer clear utility for users, as well as an adoption plan to increase their usage and adoption. Projects that solve a real problem generally have a higher chance of success.

- **Active Community :** Projects with an active community are often more promising. It's important to check if the community is active on social media, forums, and discussion platforms.

- **Communication and Transparency :** Cryptocurrency projects should be transparent in their communications with their community, including publishing regular updates on their development, partnerships, and achievements.

Taking the example of Cosmos (ATOM), this cryptocurrency is a solid project that meets several of these criteria. The Cosmos development team is strong and experienced, and they have been regularly updating on the development of their technology. Additionally, Cosmos is an interoperable blockchain that aims to connect different blockchain protocols, which can offer clear utility for users and broader adoption. Finally, Cosmos has an active community and an ecosystem of projects using its blockchain.

B. Why Diversifying Your Portfolio Is Important for Risk Reduction

The expression "don't put all your eggs in one basket" makes complete sense here and is commonly used to express caution and diversification in investments. It means that it's risky to invest everything in a single company or sector, as it can lead to a total loss if that investment fails. Therefore, it's important to diversify investments by spreading money across different projects or sectors to reduce risks and maximize the chances of success. This is particularly true in the world of cryptocurrencies, where investments are highly volatile and unpredictable. By using a diversification and risk management approach, investors can reduce their exposure to market risks and improve their long-term earning potential.

Diversifying your portfolio is important for risk reduction because it allows spreading investments across several different assets. Indeed, by investing in different types of assets such as stocks, bonds, index funds, commodities, cryptocurrencies, etc., investors can reduce the potential impact of volatility or decline in value of a single asset.

For example, if an investor only invested in stocks of a single company and that company encountered difficulties, they could lose their entire investment. On the other hand, if they had invested some of their money in stocks of different companies, bonds, index funds, etc., they would have reduced risks and potential losses in case of difficulties with a single company.

This strategy is known as portfolio diversification and is widely practiced by professional investors and renowned economists. Economists advocating diversification include Harry Markowitz, the 1990 Nobel Prize laureate in economics, who developed modern portfolio theory and demonstrated that diversification allows reducing risks without sacrificing expected returns. Benjamin Graham, the author of the classic book "The Intelligent Investor," also emphasized the importance of diversification for individual investors.

Diversification is an important strategy for investors seeking to reduce risks and maximize potential long-term returns. By investing in a variety of assets, investors can protect their portfolio against market fluctuations and unforeseen events.

Warren Buffett is another example of an investor who advocates portfolio diversification. Although known for his investments in companies such as Coca-Cola and American Express, Buffett is also a strong advocate of diversification through a variety of assets and index funds. In his famous 1993 letter to shareholders, Buffett stated, "Diversification is a protection against ignorance. It makes little sense for those who know what they're doing." He emphasized that diversification is particularly important for individual investors who cannot devote as much time and resources as professional investors to conduct in-depth research on different companies.

Buffett also recommended individual investors to diversify their portfolio through index funds, such as the S&P 500 index, which offer exposure to a wide range of companies and reduce risks associated with selecting individual stocks.

Warren Buffett is a famous investor who advocates portfolio diversification. He believes that diversification is a protection against ignorance and recommends individual investors to diversify their portfolio through a variety of assets and index funds. By following these advice, investors can reduce risks associated with selecting individual stocks and maximize long-term success chances.

C. Tips for Allocating Your Capital Among Different Cryptocurrencies and Projects

Here are some tips for allocating your capital wisely among different cryptocurrency projects :

- ❖ Diversification is key to reducing risks and maximizing chances of success. Spread your capital among different cryptocurrencies and projects to avoid putting everything into a single currency.

- ❖ Conduct thorough research on the different cryptocurrencies and projects you want to invest in. Evaluate their long-term potential, development team, adoption, and utility.

- ❖ Establish a clear investment strategy and define your long-term goals. Will you be a short-term or long-term investor?

- ❖ Evaluate the risk associated with each cryptocurrency and project and adjust your allocation accordingly. Riskier projects should represent a smaller proportion of your portfolio.

- ❖ Regularly monitor your portfolio and adjust your allocation based on market changes and your long-term goals.

By following these tips, you can allocate your capital among different cryptocurrencies and projects wisely and maximize long-term success chances.

It's important to note that capital allocation will also depend on your risk tolerance, budget, and investment experience, as mentioned in the previous point.

D. Do Your Own Research Before Investing in a Cryptocurrency

I strongly believe that it is extremely important to do your own research before investing in a new cryptocurrency. While this may seem obvious, many novice or inexperienced investors may be tempted to invest in projects that seem promising without having a thorough understanding of their fundamentals.

There are several reasons why it's important to do your own research before investing in a cryptocurrency. First, each cryptocurrency project is unique, with different characteristics, technologies, and goals. It's important to understand these differences to know if a project is viable in the long term or if it's simply a scam.

Additionally, cryptocurrency projects are often highly technical, with jargon and specific concepts to understand. Investors must take the time to familiarize themselves with these concepts and understand how they work to be able to determine the value of a project. Moreover, cryptocurrency projects are often in constant development, with regular updates and new features added. It's important to follow these developments to stay informed about the latest developments and changes in the project's outlook.

Furthermore, it's important to understand the community behind each cryptocurrency project. Community members can have a significant influence on the success or failure of a project. Therefore, investors must ensure that the community is active, engaged, and supportive of the project.

Finally, it's essential to understand the risks associated with investing in a cryptocurrency. Cryptocurrency projects are often highly volatile, with significant price fluctuations. Investors must be prepared to accept these risks and assess their risk tolerance before investing.

Investing in a cryptocurrency can be an exciting and lucrative opportunity, but it requires thorough research and a solid understanding of each project. Investors must be willing to invest time and effort to ensure they understand the fundamentals of each project before deciding to invest. By doing their own research, investors can minimize risks and make informed investment decisions. Make sure to understand its operation, utility, growth potential, and performance history.

However, despite the importance of research, some investors may still succumb to impulsive investments.

E. Investments in ICOs and STOs

ICOs and STOs, two acronyms that have stirred much debate in the cryptocurrency world. Exploring the world of Initial Coin Offerings (ICOs) and Security Token Offerings (STOs), we enter into a territory where growth opportunities can be enticing, but risks are present.

Some well-known personalities have expressed their opinions on this hot topic. For example, Tim Draper, a renowned venture capitalist, has been supportive of ICOs and has invested in several promising projects. He has recognized the potential of these fundraising methods to allow companies to innovate and finance their initiatives using cryptocurrency technology.

However, it's important to understand the advantages and risks associated with ICOs and STOs. ICOs offer the opportunity to participate in projects from their inception and to benefit from potential token value increases. They can also offer easier access to investments traditionally reserved for accredited investors. STOs, on the other hand, are regulated token offerings that offer greater security to investors due to their compliance with securities laws.

However, caution must be exercised, and best practices must be adopted to identify solid projects and avoid scams. Personalities like Andreas M. Antonopoulos, a renowned speaker and writer in the cryptocurrency field, have emphasized the importance of conducting thorough research on the teams, projects, and economic models of ICOs and STOs. It's also recommended to verify the legitimacy of projects by examining their technical documents, partnerships, and regulatory compliance.

ICOs and STOs are powerful tools for innovation and crowdfunding, but they come with significant risks. Personalities such as Gary Gensler, the chairman of the Securities and Exchange Commission (SEC) in the United States, have highlighted the need to regulate these fundraisings to protect investors from fraud and market manipulation.

During an ICO, companies typically issue digital tokens that can be purchased by investors in exchange for cryptocurrencies such as Bitcoin or Ethereum. These tokens can then be used to access the company's products or services or for speculative investments.

Among the risks associated with ICOs, vesting is an important element to consider. Vesting refers to a lock-up period during which tokens purchased during the ICO are subject to restrictions regarding their transferability or use. During this period, investors cannot freely sell, trade, or use the tokens.

Below, we identify some risks associated with vesting in the context of ICOs:

- ❖ **Lack of Liquidity** : Vesting can lead to a lack of liquidity for investors, as they cannot sell their tokens immediately after the ICO. This can lead to difficulties in quickly recovering their investment or taking advantage of investment opportunities elsewhere.

- ❖ **Price Volatility** : During the vesting period, token prices can be extremely volatile. When restrictions are lifted, and tokens become transferable, this can lead to significant price fluctuations, which can be risky for investors.

- ❖ **Project-related Risks** : Vesting can be used by project teams to incentivize investors to remain engaged in the project in the long term. However, this also means that investors bear the risk that the project may not achieve its objectives or fail altogether.

- ❖ **Governance Issues :** Vesting can lead to governance issues, as token holders who cannot yet vote or actively participate in project decisions may feel excluded from the decision-making process.

- ❖ **Beware of Tokenomics :** The term "tokenomics" is the combination of "token" and "economics." It refers to the economic structure of the project, meaning how the cryptocurrency tokens are distributed, used, and interact with the project's ecosystem. A fair and transparent distribution of tokens is essential. If a small group holds a large majority of tokens, this can create a power and influence imbalance, which may not be in the interest of investors.

It's important to note that vesting can be a useful mechanism to align the interests of investors and the project team in the long term. This can help avoid short-term speculative practices that could hinder project development. However, it's essential for investors to understand the details of vesting during an ICO and assess the associated risks before participating. Conducting thorough research on the project, its team, and its economic model is crucial for making informed investment decisions in the ICO field.

I've compiled a few examples of ICOs released in 2021 and 2022:

- ❖ **Polkadot (DOT) :** Polkadot is a multi-chain blockchain platform aimed at facilitating interoperability between different blockchains. Its ICO was conducted in 2020, and the platform became operational in 2021.

- ❖ **Solana (SOL)** : Solana is a high-performance blockchain designed for decentralized applications and smart contracts. Its ICO took place in 2020, and since then, the popularity and value of Solana have significantly increased in 2021 and 2022.

- ❖ **Avalanche (AVAX)** : Avalanche is a scalable and secure blockchain platform that aims to offer advanced features for decentralized applications. Its ICO took place in 2020, and the platform has seen increasing adoption in 2021 and 2022.
- ❖ **Filecoin (FIL)** : Filecoin is a decentralized storage network that allows users to store, retrieve, and exchange data securely. Its ICO took place in 2017, but the Filecoin network became fully operational in 2021, attracting attention due to its innovative technology.
- ❖ **Alchemy Pay (ACH)** : Alchemy Pay is a digital payment platform that facilitates cryptocurrency transactions in the real world. Its ICO took place in 2021, and the platform aims to make cryptocurrency payments more accessible and convenient.

F. Avoid Impulsive Investments, Don't Succumb to Market Panic or Excitement, and Make Informed Decisions

It is crucial to avoid impulsive investments in cryptocurrencies as they can lead to heavy financial losses. Impulsive investments are often based on emotions such as fear of missing out on an opportunity or excitement about making quick money, rather than on rational and thorough analysis of the viability and potential of each cryptocurrency project.

As economist Daniel Kahneman emphasized in his book "Thinking, Fast and Slow," humans tend to make decisions based on fast reflexes rather than taking the time to think and weigh all factors involved. Impulsive investments are thus often the result of fast thinking, which can lead to reckless and unthoughtful decisions.

Furthermore, impulsive investments in cryptocurrencies can be influenced by social media, influencers, and online comments. Investors may be tempted to follow the advice of an expert or rely on the opinion of an online crowd without taking the time to conduct their research.

A recent example of the impact of impulsive investments is the collapse of the Dogecoin cryptocurrency market in May 2021. The price of Dogecoin rose rapidly due to the currency's popularity on social media and the enthusiasm of some investors. However, the speculative bubble burst, resulting in significant losses for many investors who bought the currency at high prices.

It's important to avoid impulsive investments in cryptocurrencies and take the time to conduct thorough research before making investment decisions. Investors should also be aware of the impact of social media and the online crowd on investment decisions and focus on the fundamentals of each cryptocurrency project rather than on emotions and popular opinions.

If you missed the opportunity to invest in a particular project, don't worry. It's better to wait for the next opportunity and get on the next train rather than chasing the one you missed.

G. Be Patient, Long-Term Investments Generally Yield Better Returns Than Short-Term Investments

It is often tempting to seek short-term investments that can generate quick gains, but this can be risky and may not offer satisfactory long-term returns. Indeed, long-term investments generally yield better returns than short-term investments because they allow assets to grow and generate compound interest over a longer period.

Take the example of the stock market. According to historical data, the average annual return of the S&P 500 (a US stock market index) is about 10% since its inception in 1926. This means that investors who bought shares in the S&P 500 several decades ago and held onto their investments long-term have benefited from significant gains.

Similarly, the cryptocurrency market has also experienced significant growth over time, despite volatility. For example, Bitcoin was created in 2009, and its value has grown exponentially over the years. Although the cryptocurrency market is volatile and unpredictable in the short term, many investors believe that the underlying technology of these assets has the potential to transform the financial industry in the long term.

It's also important to note that well-known figures in the investment world, such as Warren Buffett and Peter Lynch, often recommend a long-term investment approach. Warren Buffett is famous for his long-term investment philosophy.

Understanding the term "patience" has been repeatedly emphasized in the investment process. Similarly, Peter Lynch, a former portfolio manager at Fidelity Investments, recommended investors to seek quality long-term companies rather than chasing short-term gains. Being patient and adopting a long-term investment approach can offer superior returns compared to short-term investments. Examples from the stock market and cryptocurrencies show that assets generally tend to grow over time, even though they may be volatile in the short term.

VII. Managing Emotions and Avoiding Psychological Traps

When it comes to investing in cryptocurrencies, it's easy to let emotions take over. Investors may be tempted to follow market trends, make hasty decisions based on fear or excitement, or be influenced by opinions or advice online. However, this can lead to costly mistakes and psychological traps. To succeed in cryptocurrency investments, it's important to manage emotions, make rational decisions, and follow a solid investment strategy. In this section, we'll address common psychological traps to avoid when investing in cryptocurrencies and provide practical tips for managing emotions and making sound decisions.

A. Major Psychological Traps Faced by Cryptocurrency Investors

Learn to manage your emotions; don't let fear, greed, or euphoria guide your investment decisions.

Cryptocurrency investors often face psychological traps that can jeopardize their success in the market. The first trap is greed. Investors may be tempted to chase quick gains by investing in high-risk cryptocurrencies without properly assessing the risks. This can lead to significant losses. The second trap is fear. Investors may panic and sell quickly in response to a market downturn, rather than sticking to their long-term investment strategy. The third trap is FOMO (Fear Of Missing Out), where investors may be tempted to buy popular cryptocurrencies due to fear of missing out on profit opportunities, even if it may not be a rational decision.

The fourth trap is the influence of others. Investors may be influenced by online opinions or advice, even if it doesn't align with their own investment strategy. The fifth trap is overconfidence, where investors may be overly confident in their investment skills and take unnecessary risks. Finally, the sixth trap is information overload, where investors may be overwhelmed by the amount of information available online and make decisions based on incorrect or incomplete data. It's important for cryptocurrency investors to recognize these common psychological traps and take steps to avoid them. This may include developing a long-term investment strategy, investing only in cryptocurrencies they understand and trust, and using tools such as stop-loss orders to limit losses in case of market downturns.

It's important to take the time to carefully evaluate all information before making an investment decision and not be influenced by the opinions or advice of others. By following these practical tips, cryptocurrency investors can avoid psychological traps and increase their chances of success in the market.

An example of a psychological trap in the cryptocurrency market is information overload and overconfidence, which can lead to impulsive investment decisions. A well-known case is that of James Howells, a British IT worker who mined 7,500 Bitcoins in 2009 but stored them on his laptop, which was eventually thrown away. When he realized his mistake, he attempted to retrieve the hard drive, but to no avail. However, Howells continued to monitor the cryptocurrency market and follow the news, hoping that the value of Bitcoin would increase enough for him to recover his loss.

In 2013, Bitcoin reached historic highs, and James Howells began to feel confident in his market growth predictions. However, his excessive confidence in his investment skills led him to make a hasty and emotional decision: he sold all his other investments to buy more Bitcoins, hoping to recover his loss. Unfortunately, the value of Bitcoin eventually plummeted, leaving Howells with significant losses. His story is a poignant example of the importance of making investment decisions based on rational analysis rather than emotions and irrational forecasts.

Now that we've seen common psychological traps in the cryptocurrency market, it's important to discuss how to manage emotions and avoid making impulsive decisions.

B. How to Manage Emotions and Avoid Making Impulsive Decisions

Managing your emotions is essential for making wise investment decisions in the cryptocurrency market. Rapid price fluctuations and erratic movements can be stressful and trigger emotional reactions such as fear, greed, and anxiety. Therefore, it's crucial to take steps to avoid making impulsive decisions that can harm your portfolio.

A first step in managing your emotions is to step back and keep a long-term perspective. Cryptocurrency markets are known to be volatile and unpredictable in the short term, but historically, they have shown an upward trend in the long term. Thus, it's important not to be overly reactive to short-term fluctuations and keep your long-term goals in mind.

Another strategy for managing emotions is to establish strict rules for your portfolio and follow them disciplined. This may include limits for purchases and sales, as well as maximum percentages for each cryptocurrency. By following strict rules, you avoid making impulsive decisions based on momentary emotions.

Another effective strategy is to take regular breaks to allow yourself to relax and decompress. Cryptocurrency markets can be very stressful, especially when prices fluctuate rapidly. Taking time for yourself can help reduce stress and make more thoughtful decisions. Finally, it's important to maintain open and honest communication with yourself and your surroundings. Talking about your concerns and fears can help you better understand your emotions and make more rational decisions.

By keeping honest and open communication, you can avoid making impulsive decisions based on negative emotions.

In summary, managing emotions is an essential part of investing in the cryptocurrency market. By maintaining a long-term perspective, establishing strict rules, taking regular breaks, and maintaining honest and open communication, you can avoid making impulsive decisions that could harm your portfolio.

C. Tips for Maintaining a Healthy and Optimistic Mindset Despite Market Fluctuations

In the cryptocurrency market, price fluctuations are common. It's easy to become anxious or pessimistic when prices fall or euphoric and excited when they rise. However, it's important to maintain a healthy and optimistic mindset to make good investment decisions.

First and foremost, it's important to remember that markets are cyclical and tend to move in cycles of ups and downs. Investors with a long-term perspective can easily overcome short-term fluctuations and achieve their long-term financial goals.

Next, it's important to stay informed and continue learning about cryptocurrencies. Investors with a deep understanding of cryptocurrency fundamentals can make informed decisions and have a better understanding of market trends.

It's also crucial to keep emotions under control. Investors should avoid making impulsive decisions based on fear, greed, or euphoria. Emotion can often be an enemy of reason, and investors should be aware of their own emotional biases.

Finally, it's important to stay positive and maintain an optimistic attitude. Investors should focus on their long-term goals and be prepared to overcome short-term obstacles. Investors who maintain a positive attitude and long-term perspective tend to succeed in the long run.

In summary, to maintain a healthy and optimistic mindset despite market fluctuations, it's important to maintain a long-term perspective, stay informed, keep emotions under control, and remain positive. Investors who follow these tips have a good chance of succeeding in the cryptocurrency market.

D. Don't Bet More Than You Can Afford to Lose

Invest only the money you can afford to lose without compromising your financial security and mental well-being.

One of the most important rules of cryptocurrency investing is never to invest more than you can afford to lose. This may seem obvious, but many inexperienced investors succumb to the temptation to bet big in hopes of making quick gains. However, this can quickly turn into a financial disaster, especially if the market turns against you.

Therefore, it's crucial to establish a solid and realistic investment strategy that takes into account your financial resources, investment goals, and risk tolerance. It's also important never to invest money earmarked for significant expenses, such as bill payments or tuition fees.

It's also important to diversify your cryptocurrency investment portfolio. By not putting all your eggs in one basket, you can minimize risks and maximize opportunities for gains. It's recommended to allocate a percentage of your portfolio to different cryptocurrencies based on their growth potential and level of risk.

Keep in mind that cryptocurrency investing is a long-term game. Short-term fluctuations are inevitable, but if you invest responsibly and maintain a healthy mindset, you can achieve significant gains in the long run. Don't be distracted by short-term news and market events, and always keep your long-term investment goals in mind.

E. Understanding Market Cycle Psychology

The psychology of a market cycle is a complex concept that seeks to understand the emotional and behavioral reactions of investors and financial market participants throughout an economic cycle. This cycle typically consists of four main phases: expansion, peak, contraction, and trough. Each phase has distinct psychological characteristics that influence investment decisions and market participants' behaviors.

During the expansion phase, also known as the bullish phase or boom, optimism is at its peak. Positive economic news, such as strong economic growth, rising corporate profits, and general confidence in the economy, fuel investors' euphoria. At this stage, investors' psychology is often characterized by risk appetite, overconfidence, and fear of missing out on profit opportunities. This attitude can lead to excessive buying behavior, overestimation of assets, and neglect of potential risks.

As the market reaches its peak, the second phase of the cycle, investors' psychology begins to change. Signs of an overvalued market and early signs of economic slowdown can lead to some caution. Investors may start taking profits, reducing their risk exposure, and becoming more selective in their investment decisions. Confidence may still be relatively high, but the first cracks in positive sentiment begin to appear.

The third phase, contraction, marks the beginning of the market correction. Economic news deteriorates, corporate profits begin to decline, and concerns about overall economic health become more prominent. Investors' psychology shifts from optimism to caution, even fear. Anxiety and uncertainty set in, which can lead to massive asset sales, increased volatility, and a flight to safer assets, such as government bonds. Investors may feel frustration, dejection, and confusion about the best way to protect their capital.

Finally, the trough phase, also known as the depression phase, occurs when the market reaches its lowest level. Investors' psychology is generally characterized by fear, panic, and extreme pessimism. Economic news is negative, confidence is low, and investors may be tempted to completely withdraw from the market. However, some savvy investors may see this phase as a buying opportunity, anticipating a future recovery. The psychology of these investors differs from the majority, as they are willing to take risks and deviate from the consensus.

The "**Wall ST Cheat Sheet**" market cycle chart is a tool that represents the different phases through which a market goes over time. It helps visualize price fluctuations, transaction volumes, and overall economic activity.

This chart is often used to analyze economic trends and cycles, as well as to make informed investment decisions. It typically consists of eight main phases :

- ➢ **Disbelief :** Disbelief occurs when investors struggle to accept an economic reality or market situation. This can happen when unexpected events or crises occur, and investors may refuse to admit the severity of the situation, which can lead to underestimation of risks.

- ➢ **Hope :** Hope is an emotional state that often occurs after a period of contraction or prolonged market decline. Investors begin to perceive signs of potential recovery and hope for future gains. However, hope can be fragile and vulnerable to reversals.

- ➢ **Optimism** : Optimism is an emotional state characterized by confidence and positive expectations about the future market trend. Optimistic investors believe in continued economic growth, improved corporate profits, and favorable prospects. This can lead to increased risk appetite and bolder investment decisions.

- ➢ **Belief :** Belief refers to an emotional state in which investors have strong conviction about the future direction of the market. They may firmly believe in a specific trend or investment thesis and act accordingly. This can lead to investment behaviors focused on confirming this belief.

- ➢ **Thrill** : Thrill occurs when investors are caught in a feeling of excitement and anticipation due to rapid market movements. This can happen when there is high volatility or significant price fluctuations, which can trigger emotional excitement among active investors seeking to profit from these movements.

- ➢ **Euphoria** : Euphoria is an intense emotional state of happiness and excessive excitement that can occur during a period of strong market growth. Investors may be overwhelmed by a sense of euphoria and tend to overestimate the positive prospects of the market, which can lead to irrational speculative behaviors.

- ➢ **Complacency** : Complacency occurs when investors become overly confident and neglect potential risks. This can happen after a prolonged period of market growth, when investors assume that good performance will continue indefinitely, leading to imprudent decisions and ignoring warning signs.

- ➢ **Anxiety** : Anxiety is an emotional state characterized by worry, tension, and apprehension about the future market trend. Anxious investors may experience a high level of stress and uncertainty.

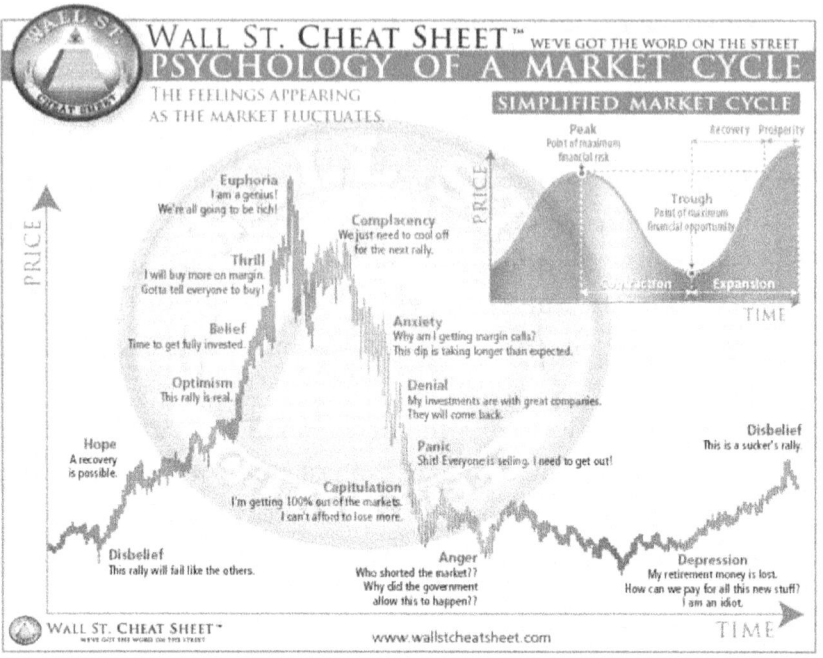

Comparing the price of Bitcoin with the "Wall Street Cheat Sheet" curve offers an interesting perspective on the similarities and differences between these two entities. While Bitcoin is volatile, subject to significant fluctuations due to various factors such as adoption, regulation, and market news, the "Wall Street Cheat Sheet" curve represents the general phases of the traditional financial market.

When overlaying the price of Bitcoin on the "Wall Street Cheat Sheet" curve, parallels can be observed with the emotions and behaviors of investors. The "Bull Market" phases of Bitcoin, characterized by periods of sustained price increases, could be compared to the rise of hope and optimism in the traditional market. Similarly, Bitcoin's "Bear Market" periods, with significant price declines, could reflect the disillusionment and despair represented in the "Wall Street Cheat Sheet" curve.

Comparing Bitcoin to the "Wall Street Cheat Sheet" curve can offer an intriguing visual perspective on price movements and market emotions.

F. Market Manipulation

It is crucial to remain vigilant in the face of discourse surrounding Bitcoin and cryptocurrencies, especially when major players like Grayscale or BlackRock express criticism. In many cases, these comments could be influenced by hidden interests aiming to manipulate the market in their favor. The cryptocurrency environment is known for its volatility and sensitivity to news, making it a prime target for manipulation tactics.

When significant entities criticize Bitcoin and cryptocurrencies, it is essential to adopt a cautious and analytical approach. These criticisms may be used as a means to sow doubt among less informed investors, thereby prompting "weak hands" to sell their holdings. This can lead to price declines and allow large entities to repurchase at lower prices, thus strengthening their position.

Market manipulation can take various forms, from spreading false information to alarmist comments in traditional media or on social networks. Investors must be aware of these strategies and adopt a critical approach to any information. It is best to rely on reliable sources, follow long-term trends, and maintain a global perspective.

Ultimately, investing in cryptocurrencies requires a thorough understanding of the market and a cautious assessment of information. Relying on verified sources and having a solid understanding of the fundamentals can help minimize the risks associated with market manipulation.

VIII. Following News and Market Trends

Following news and market trends is crucial for cryptocurrency investors looking to maximize their profits. The cryptocurrency market is volatile and constantly evolving, so it is important to stay informed about recent developments, important announcements, and market trends. This allows for informed decision-making and seizing profit opportunities.

Indeed, by closely monitoring news and market trends, investors can detect signs of cryptocurrency price increases or decreases, allowing them to buy or sell accordingly. In this section, we will explore how to effectively follow news and market trends in the cryptocurrency market.

A. Why It's Important to Follow News and Market Trends

It is crucial to follow news and market trends in the cryptocurrency market for several reasons. First and foremost, the cryptocurrency market is a volatile, constantly evolving market influenced by various factors such as economic news, political events, regulatory decisions, new technologies, etc. By staying informed about news and market trends, investors can make more informed and strategic investment decisions.

Furthermore, by following market trends, investors can detect signs of cryptocurrency price increases or decreases, allowing them to make buying or selling decisions accordingly. For example, if a cryptocurrency experiences an increase in value due to an important announcement or a bullish trend, investors may decide to buy this cryptocurrency before the price rises even further. Similarly, if a bearish trend emerges, investors may decide to sell their position before the cryptocurrency's value decreases further.

Finally, by following news and market trends, investors can stay informed about technological developments and innovations that may impact the cryptocurrency market. This can help them identify cryptocurrencies with long-term potential that could become profitable investments in the future.

In summary, following news and market trends is a crucial aspect of cryptocurrency investing. It allows investors to make more informed and strategic decisions, detect signs of cryptocurrency price increases or decreases, and stay informed about technological developments and innovations in the field.

B. How to Stay Informed and Identify Investment Opportunities

To stay informed about news and market trends in the cryptocurrency market, there are several sources of information available. Cryptocurrency-focused media outlets such as Coindesk, Coin Telegraph, and CryptoSlate are reliable sources for up-to-date information on major market events. Social media platforms are also a valuable tool for following thought leaders and influential personalities in the cryptocurrency industry (including Twitter, Telegram, Discord, etc.).

Additionally, it is important to monitor trends and technological developments in the industry. For example, the announcement of blockchain adoption by a large company may indicate a bullish trend for associated cryptocurrencies. Strategic partnerships between cryptocurrency companies and traditional businesses may also indicate promising investment opportunities.

It is also important to monitor regulations and laws regarding cryptocurrencies in different countries. New regulations can have a significant impact on cryptocurrency prices and investment opportunities (such as the MICA project in Europe or upcoming strict regulations in the USA, Japan's opening to the crypto market, etc.).

Finally, the cryptocurrency investor community can also provide valuable information on trends and investment opportunities. Online forums, social media discussion groups, and cryptocurrency events are places where investors share their knowledge and experiences, which can be useful for identifying trends and investment opportunities.

Following news and market trends in the cryptocurrency market is crucial for investors, as it can help them identify promising investment opportunities. The available sources of information are varied, ranging from specialized media to online communities, and it is important to use them to stay informed and make informed investment decisions.

C. Tips for Avoiding Fake News and Unreliable Information Sources

In the digital world, false or misleading information spreads quickly, and it can be difficult to know what is true and what is not. When it comes to cryptocurrency investments, it is crucial to avoid unreliable sources of information and focus on relevant and accurate information. To do this, it is important to follow recognized and quality sources of information.

To start, it is recommended to focus on well-established and reliable financial media outlets such as Bloomberg, BFM Business, Journal du Coin, Cryptoast, Cryptonaute, Coindesk, Forbes. These sources of information are regularly updated and provide accurate and objective analysis of the latest developments in the cryptocurrency market.

It is also important to follow the official accounts of cryptocurrency projects on social media. Projects regularly post updates on their activities, upcoming developments, partnerships, and other relevant information that may impact the price of their cryptocurrency.

Finally, it is important to verify sources and ensure that the information comes from a reliable source. Experts recommend being skeptical of sensational information or unfounded rumors and taking the time to fact-check before making an investment decision.

Experts such as Peter Mallouk, president of Creative Planning, also recommend seeking professional financial advisors to help filter information and make informed investment decisions. It is important to choose a competent and experienced financial advisor who has a deep understanding of the cryptocurrency market and appropriate investment strategies.

D. Use Reliable Exchange Platforms: Choose Reputable Platforms to Avoid Scams and Hacks

Using reliable and reputable exchange platforms is crucial to avoid scams and hacks. Unfortunately, cryptocurrency investors have been victims of many scams in recent years. Hackers often target the least secure exchange platforms, and fund thefts are common. Reliable exchange platforms support the security of your funds by using cold storage systems to protect their clients' assets. Additionally, they conduct rigorous checks to ensure transaction security and personal data protection.

However, not all exchanges are created equal. It is essential to choose a platform that has proven itself, has a good reputation in the industry, and is approved by regulatory authorities. The most popular and reliable exchanges on the market include Binance, Coinbase, Kraken, among others. They all have a strong reputation and have proven their reliability over the years.

Cryptocurrency investors should also beware of offers that seem too good to be true, such as promotions promising high and quick returns. These promises are often a sign of a potential scam. It is important never to give your personal information or private keys to anyone. Scams and hacks are real risks, but by choosing a reliable exchange platform, you can minimize these risks and invest confidently in cryptocurrencies.

In recent years, decentralized exchange platforms (DEXs) have gained popularity among cryptocurrency investors. Unlike centralized exchange platforms, DEXs are not controlled by a company or organization, but rather by decentralized peer-to-peer networks. This means that transactions are conducted directly between parties without the intermediary of a central entity, reducing the risks of hacking or data theft.

Among the most popular DEXs are Uniswap, PancakeSwap, Curve, DYDX, GMX, VELA, or Kromatika finance. These platforms offer advantages such as security, privacy, and decentralization, as well as transaction fees often lower than those of centralized platforms. Additionally, DEXs offer greater accessibility to a wider range of tokens, allowing investors to explore new investment opportunities.

However, it is important to note that DEXs also present risks, particularly regarding the liquidity and price volatility of assets. Investors must be prepared to conduct their own research and understand the risks associated with DEXs before making investment decisions.

IX. Emerging Trends in the World of Cryptocurrencies : Perspectives and Narratives for the Future

As the cryptocurrency market continues to gain popularity and generate increasing interest, new trends and narratives are emerging, providing insight into the prospects for the years to come. In this introduction, we will explore some of the main trends that have been discussed in the field of cryptocurrencies, as well as the narratives that could shape the landscape of this dynamic industry. From questions related to institutional adoption and CBDCs (Central Bank Digital Currencies) to the evolution of regulation and exciting developments in decentralized finance (DeFi), we invite you to embark on a captivating journey within the constantly evolving cryptocurrency ecosystem. Get ready to discover the challenges, opportunities, and perspectives that could define the exciting future of this financial revolution.

Here are some trends and narratives in the field of cryptocurrencies for the years to come :

- ✓ **Increased Institutional Adoption :** More financial institutions, companies, and institutional investors are expected to integrate cryptocurrencies into their investment strategies and operations. The arrival of major institutional players could contribute to broader adoption and increased legitimacy of cryptocurrencies.

- ✓ **CBDC Development :** Central Bank Digital Currencies (CBDCs) are cryptocurrencies issued by central banks. Many countries are actively studying and experimenting with the creation of their CBDCs, which could have a significant impact on the global monetary and financial landscape.

- ✓ **Integration of Blockchain into Traditional Sectors :** Blockchain technology is increasingly being adopted in various sectors such as finance, healthcare, logistics, real estate, etc. The integration of blockchain could bring more transparency, efficiency, and security to these areas.

- ✓ **DeFi Development :** Decentralized Finance (DeFi) continues to grow and attract attention. DeFi protocols enable intermediary-free financial services and open up new investment, lending, and trading opportunities.

- ✓ **Regulatory Evolution :** Regulators worldwide will continue to monitor and adapt their regulatory frameworks for cryptocurrencies. Clearer and more stable regulation could promote institutional adoption and investment.

- ✓ **Environmental Sustainability :** The issue of energy consumption related to mining certain cryptocurrencies, such as Bitcoin, is attracting increasing attention. There could be greater demand for cryptocurrencies with a low carbon footprint.

A. Institutional Adoption

Increased institutional adoption is one of the most striking elements of the current cryptocurrency landscape. Over the past few years, we have witnessed a significant transition, where financial institutions, companies, and institutional investors have begun to integrate cryptocurrencies into their investment strategies and operations. This evolution marks a major turning point for cryptocurrencies, as it brings increased credibility and legitimacy to an ecosystem that was once considered marginal and reserved for insiders.

Several factors have contributed to this growing institutional adoption. Firstly, the increasing recognition of cryptocurrencies as a distinct and diversified asset class has attracted the attention of fund managers and institutional investors seeking new investment opportunities. Low interest rates in the traditional economy have also led many investors to seek higher returns in assets with high growth potential, and cryptocurrencies have attracted attention as an alternative.

Furthermore, the improvement of infrastructure and the maturity of the cryptocurrency market have made access easier for financial institutions. Safer and regulated exchanges, secure custody solutions, and advanced analytics tools have been developed to meet the specific needs of institutional players. Innovations in security and compliance standards have also helped reassure institutional investors and reduce the risks associated with cryptocurrencies.

As a result, many financial institutions have begun to allocate a portion of their assets under management to cryptocurrencies, either by investing directly in digital assets such as Bitcoin and Ethereum or by exposing themselves through cryptocurrency-backed financial products. Investment funds, insurance companies, pension funds, and even some banks have joined the movement, actively participating in the evolution of the market.

Increased institutional adoption has also paved the way for new opportunities for cryptocurrency projects. Blockchain startups and innovative projects now benefit from institutional investor interest, which could accelerate the development of disruptive technologies and the integration of blockchain into various industries.

However, despite this positive development, some questions and challenges remain. The inherent volatility of cryptocurrencies and the lack of clear regulation in some countries may pose obstacles for financial institutions seeking to further engage in this space. Uncertainties surrounding security, compliance, and consumer protection issues need to be addressed to further strengthen confidence in the market.

Overall, increased institutional adoption represents an important step in the maturation of the cryptocurrency market. This trend could continue to shape the future of this expanding ecosystem by bridging the gap between traditional markets and the new frontiers of decentralized finance. However, it is essential for stakeholders to remain vigilant to potential risks and collaborate to build a sustainable and balanced environment that fosters growth and innovation in this emerging and promising field.

B. Development of CBDCs

The development of Central Bank Digital Currencies (CBDCs) represents a major evolution in the global monetary and financial landscape. As cryptocurrencies have attracted increasing interest in recent years, central banks around the world have begun to explore the possibility of creating their own digital currencies. These initiatives aim to modernize payment systems, promote financial inclusion, and strengthen economic stability in an increasingly digitized financial transactions context.

The underlying principle is similar between CBDCs and cryptocurrencies, as they are both digital currencies. However, CBDCs are issued and regulated by central banks, giving them a different status and role compared to decentralized cryptocurrencies like Bitcoin. CBDCs could coexist with traditional fiat currencies and serve as a digital representation of national currencies.

Several countries have already initiated research and pilot projects to explore the feasibility of CBDCs. The motivations behind these initiatives vary, but common objectives include improving payment efficiency, reducing transaction costs, combating financial crime, and enhancing monetary policy effectiveness.

The development of CBDCs has the potential to revolutionize the global financial system in several ways. Firstly, CBDCs could facilitate faster and cheaper cross-border transactions, improving financial inclusion and reducing the reliance on intermediaries such as correspondent banks. Secondly, CBDCs could enhance the effectiveness of monetary policy by providing central banks with more direct control over the money supply and circulation. Finally, CBDCs could promote innovation in payment systems and financial services, fostering competition and driving efficiency gains.

However, the development of CBDCs also raises important questions and challenges. Technical considerations such as scalability, security, and interoperability need to be addressed to ensure the smooth operation of CBDC systems. Regulatory issues related to data privacy, consumer protection, and anti-money laundering measures also need to be carefully considered to mitigate potential risks and ensure compliance with existing regulations.

The development of CBDCs represents a significant milestone in the ongoing digitization of the global economy. While the full impact of CBDCs remains to be seen, they have the potential to reshape the financial landscape and improve the efficiency, accessibility, and inclusivity of financial services. However, the successful implementation of CBDCs will require close collaboration between central banks, regulators, financial institutions, and technology providers to address technical, regulatory, and operational challenges effectively.

The underlying principle is similar between cryptocurrencies and CBDCs, as they are both digital, but the fundamental difference lies in their centralization or decentralization. A CBDC is a centralized digital currency issued by a central bank with associated control and regulation.

As an evolved version of traditional fiat currency issued by central banks, a CBDC is supposed to offer a more secure framework, backed by a major institution such as our elites. Consequently, this reduces the risk of bankruptcy since it is not issued by a private entity. Moreover, it attempts to temporarily solve the volatility problem commonly found in most cryptocurrencies.

However, as a fiat currency, a CBDC is subject to a key characteristic: the central bank can increase the supply of CBDC as much as it wants. Therefore, a CBDC does not solve the inflation problem related to money creation, unlike bitcoin, whose supply is limited by a specific algorithm.

The development of CBDCs has been motivated by several factors. Firstly, the rapid evolution of payment technologies and the increasing popularity of digital payments have prompted central banks to contemplate the future of national currencies in an increasingly digital environment. CBDCs could offer benefits such as faster transaction speeds, 24/7 availability, and reduced costs associated with issuing and managing cash.

Moreover, CBDCs could improve financial inclusion by allowing more people to access financial services. CBDCs could be accessible to everyone, including the unbanked population, by removing traditional barriers such as the need for a bank account to conduct transactions.

Furthermore, CBDCs could enhance financial stability by providing a safe and stable alternative to private cryptocurrencies, which are sometimes subject to extreme volatility. Central banks could also use CBDCs as a tool to better control monetary policy and regulate the economy, especially in times of financial crises.

Due to their potential importance, many countries have launched pilot projects and experiments to explore the possibilities offered by CBDCs. The People's Bank of China has been one of the pioneers in conducting trials of its central bank digital currency, the digital yuan. Other central banks, including those of Sweden, Canada, the United Kingdom, and many other countries, have also announced their plans to study and experiment with CBDCs.

However, despite these promising developments, the full deployment of CBDCs also raises significant challenges. Issues related to privacy, security, data protection, and protection against cyberattacks need to be addressed. The implications for monetary policy, financial stability, and international relations also need to be carefully evaluated.

C. Integration of Blockchain in Traditional Sectors

The integration of blockchain into traditional sectors represents a major trend that is rapidly transforming how we conceive and manage existing systems and processes. Blockchain, as the underlying technology of cryptocurrencies, offers significant advantages in terms of transparency, security, traceability, and efficiency. This decentralized technology allows for the immutable recording and verification of transactions and data, paving the way for innovative applications in various fields.

In the financial sector, the integration of blockchain has given rise to decentralized finance (DeFi), a new approach to finance that eliminates traditional intermediaries such as banks and brokers. DeFi protocols enable peer-to-peer lending, trading, and direct investments, offering opportunities for access to financial services without permission and without geographical discrimination.

In the logistics and supply chain sector, blockchain offers a solution for tracking and verifying products at every stage of their journey. Companies can use distributed ledgers to ensure the authenticity, provenance, and quality of products, thereby enhancing consumer trust and reducing the risks of counterfeiting.

In the healthcare sector, the integration of blockchain allows for the secure and efficient sharing of patients' medical records while protecting their privacy. Healthcare professionals can access accurate and up-to-date information, improving diagnoses and treatments while reducing medical errors.

The real estate sector also benefits from blockchain by simplifying property transactions and facilitating global real estate investment. Through smart contracts, real estate transactions can be automated and secured, eliminating the costs and delays associated with traditional processes.

Furthermore, blockchain is used in the energy sector to facilitate the management of decentralized electricity networks, in the arts sector to ensure the authenticity and traceability of artworks, and even in public administration to improve the efficiency of government services.

However, despite these benefits, the integration of blockchain into traditional sectors is not without challenges. Implementing new infrastructures and governance standards can be complex, and data security must be rigorously considered to avoid breaches and hacking. Moreover, the acceptance and regulation of blockchain technology vary from country to country, requiring international collaboration to promote its widespread adoption.

The integration of blockchain into traditional sectors offers significant opportunities to improve the efficiency, security, and transparency of existing processes. By enabling the creation of decentralized systems, blockchain paves the way for a new era of innovation and transformation in diverse fields such as finance, logistics, healthcare, real estate, and many others. However, to fully realize the potential of this technology, concerted efforts are needed to address implementation and regulatory challenges while establishing governance standards that promote responsible and sustainable adoption.

D. Development of DeFi

The development of DeFi (Decentralized Finance) represents a revolution in the traditional financial world. DeFi is a blockchain-based ecosystem that allows for the creation and provision of a range of financial services without the use of intermediaries such as banks or brokers. This new decentralized approach aims to democratize access to financial services by allowing anyone with an internet connection to access financial products previously reserved for insiders.

At the heart of DeFi are "smart contracts," which are self-executing autonomous programs that operate according to predefined conditions. These smart contracts are essential for creating DeFi platforms where transactions and financial agreements are automatically executed without human intervention.

DeFi applications offer a diverse range of services, including peer-to-peer lending and borrowing, liquidity pools, decentralized exchanges (DEX), and savings and yield products. For example, users can deposit their cryptocurrencies into DeFi lending protocols and earn interest on their deposits. These savings and yield products are often open to all without the need for complex identification or verification. (AAVE on the Ethereum blockchain or HATOM on the Elrond blockchain, OSMOSIS on the Cosmos blockchain, for example).

The development of DeFi has been facilitated by the emergence of blockchain platforms and protocols such as Ethereum, which provide an environment conducive to creating smart contracts. Interoperability between different DeFi protocols also allows for seamless integration and continuous growth of the ecosystem.

DeFi has experienced explosive growth in recent years, attracting the attention of investors, businesses, and even governments. However, despite its disruptive potential, DeFi is not without challenges. Security is a major concern, as vulnerabilities in smart contracts can lead to significant fund losses. Cases of hacks and protocol vulnerabilities have been reported, highlighting the need to improve the security and resilience of DeFi applications.

Regulation is another challenge for the development of DeFi. Financial authorities are seeking to understand and regulate this new ecosystem to protect consumers and prevent illegal activities. A balanced approach is needed to enable innovation while ensuring the safety and protection of users.

Despite these challenges, DeFi continues to garner growing enthusiasm, attracting millions of users and billions of dollars' worth of value locked in its protocols. Its potential to disrupt and democratize traditional financial services is drawing attention from investors and entrepreneurs worldwide.

The development of DeFi is fundamentally changing how we perceive and access financial services. By harnessing the power of blockchain and smart contracts, DeFi offers exciting opportunities for unprecedented financial inclusion, efficiency, and accessibility. However, to fully realize its potential, concerted efforts are needed to strengthen security, improve interoperability, and establish a balanced regulatory framework. DeFi is an ongoing revolution that promises to reshape the future of finance on a global scale.

E. Digital Identity

Digital identity has become an increasingly relevant and crucial topic as we move towards an increasingly digitized society. Digital identity refers to the set of information and attributes that uniquely identify an individual in the digital world. It encompasses a wide range of personal data, from basic information such as name, age, and address, to fingerprints, voiceprints, and even biometric data.

The rapid evolution of technology, particularly blockchain and cryptography, has opened new perspectives for managing and protecting digital identity. Digital identity systems based on blockchain can offer high levels of security, privacy, and decentralization. These systems enable individuals to control their own personal data and decide which information they want to share with third parties, while ensuring its integrity and immutability.

Digital identity has many advantages and applications in various sectors. In the financial domain, it can facilitate access to online banking services, thereby enabling increased financial inclusion for the unbanked or those living in remote areas. In healthcare, it can facilitate access to electronic medical records and enhance the privacy of patients' sensitive information.

Digital identity can also play a crucial role in combating fraud and identity theft by offering safer means of authenticating users online. Authentication processes based on biometric technologies, such as facial recognition and fingerprinting, can significantly enhance the security of digital transactions and interactions.

However, despite its benefits, digital identity also raises concerns regarding privacy protection and data security. Massive collection and storage of personal data can expose individuals to risks of privacy breaches and identity theft. Therefore, it is essential to establish robust security protocols and mechanisms for informed consent to ensure the protection of personal information.

Moreover, the issue of centralization and control of digital identity systems sparks debates about data sovereignty. It is crucial to strike a balance between security and efficiency while preserving individuals' rights to privacy and self-determination.

Digital identity is a fundamental aspect of our growing digital life. It offers exciting opportunities to facilitate access to services, enhance transaction security, and protect personal data. However, its development must be approached with caution, paying special attention to security, privacy, and the protection of individual rights. The future of digital identity will depend on how successfully we create balanced, privacy-respecting, and secure systems, while enabling individuals to control their own data in an ever-evolving digital world.

F. Real World Assets

Real World Assets (RWAs) in the cryptocurrency world represent an exciting evolution of the blockchain ecosystem. Unlike purely digital cryptocurrencies, these assets are backed by tangible real-world assets such as real estate, commodities, artwork, stocks, and more. The concept of RWAs is at the core of asset tokenization, which aims to digitize and fractionate traditional assets to make them accessible on blockchains. This sector is rapidly growing and is expected to be a major player in the upcoming BullRun of 2024-2025.

> **Birth of RWAs** : RWAs emerged in response to the need to create bridges between the digital world of cryptocurrencies and the physical world of tangible assets. This convergence has opened new possibilities for investment, crowdfunding, and liquidity.

> **Asset Tokenization** : Tokenization is the process of converting real-world assets into digital tokens on a blockchain. These tokens represent ownership of a fraction of the underlying asset, facilitating trading and division of assets into smaller units.

> **Advantages of RWAs** : RWAs offer greater accessibility to investors worldwide, as they enable investment in assets that were previously reserved for large investors. Additionally, blockchain ensures transparency, traceability, and security of transactions.

> **Tokenized Real Estate** : Real estate is one of the most promising sectors for RWAs. Investors can purchase fractions of real estate properties, reducing entry costs and offering greater diversification.

> **Commodities and Artwork** : Commodities such as gold, silver, oil, as well as high-value artwork, can also be tokenized. This creates new opportunities for collectors and investors.

> **Financial Markets** : RWAs are disrupting traditional financial markets. Stocks, bonds, and investment funds are now available in token form, offering increased liquidity and 24/7 trading opportunities.

> **Increasing Adoption** : RWAs are rapidly gaining popularity, and

more and more companies and projects are venturing into asset tokenization. Regulators are also adapting their legal frameworks to accommodate this new asset class.

- **Regulatory Challenges** : Despite enthusiasm, RWAs face regulatory challenges. Authorities seek to protect investors while fostering innovation. Clear regulatory frameworks are essential for the long-term development of these assets.

- **Interconnectivity of Blockchains** : The future of RWAs lies in the interconnectivity of blockchains. Projects aim to create bridges between different blockchains to enable free movement of RWAs.

- **DeFi and RWAs** : Decentralized Finance (DeFi) greatly benefits from RWAs, allowing token holders to access loans, staking, and other financial services without intermediaries.

- **Financial Inclusion** : RWAs can open up financial inclusion opportunities for populations previously excluded from traditional markets.

- **Asset Fractionalization** : RWAs enable the fractionalization of assets into smaller units, widening the potential investor base.

- **Transaction Automation** : Through smart contract technology, transactions related to RWAs can be automated, reducing costs and delays.

- **Decentralized Governance** : Some RWA projects incorporate decentralized governance mechanisms, allowing token holders to participate in decisions regarding the management of the underlying asset.

- **The Role of Oracles:** Oracles are systems that feed real-world data into blockchains, which is essential for RWAs that depend on accurate information about underlying assets.

> **Insurance and Assurance :** The insurance industry is growing to offer coverage against risks associated with RWAs, such as property damage or loss of value of tokenized assets.

> **Technological Evolution :** Technological advancements, such as blockchain scaling and improved security, will play a key role in the widespread adoption of RWAs.

> **Investor Education :** Educating investors about the nature of RWAs, associated risks, and benefits is essential for successful adoption.

> **Protection of Property Rights :** Blockchain technology offers undeniable property guarantees, but legal challenges remain in case of disputes.

> **Combination with Other Technologies :** RWAs can be combined with other emerging technologies, such as artificial intelligence and the Internet of Things, to create even richer ecosystems.

Real World Assets have the potential to fundamentally transform how we invest, trade, and access real-world assets. With evolving regulations, improving technologies, and increasing adoption, the future of RWAs is promising, paving the way for a more inclusive and transparent financial economy. Investors, innovators, and regulators are working hand in hand to shape this future, where the boundary between the digital world and the real world continues to blur.

Mastering Bitcoin and Cryptocurrencies : A Comprehensive Guide for Beginners

X. Bonus : The Guide to Thoughtful Investment

A. CRYPTO CARDS

Owning a crypto card that offers cashback in cryptocurrency presents several attractive advantages for users interested in both traditional payments and the cryptocurrency ecosystem. Here are some reasons why such a card can be appealing:

1. **Accumulation of Digital Assets :** Cashback in cryptocurrency allows users to accumulate digital assets through their daily expenses. Instead of simply receiving cash or reward points, users receive cryptocurrency, which has the potential to increase in value over time. It provides an indirect way to invest in cryptocurrency markets while conducting routine transactions.

2. **Portfolio Diversification :** Owning cryptocurrencies can be an effective diversification strategy for investments. By receiving small amounts of different cryptocurrencies through cashback, users can expand their portfolio beyond traditional assets.

3. **Exposure to the Cryptocurrency Market :** For those interested in cryptocurrencies but hesitant to invest large sums of money, cashback in cryptocurrency offers an opportunity to enter the market without spending additional money.

4. **Participation in the Crypto Ecosystem :** By using a card that offers cashback in cryptocurrency, users indirectly contribute to the adoption and use of cryptocurrencies in daily commerce. This can further stimulate the acceptance of cryptocurrencies as a means of payment.

5. **Tax Benefits :** Depending on the jurisdiction and local tax laws, purchasing goods and services with cashback-derived cryptocurrencies could have tax benefits, such as more favorable regulations for cryptocurrency transactions.

6. **Potential for Gains :** If the cryptocurrency received as cashback increases in value, users could realize potential gains by selling the cryptocurrency at an opportune time.

7. **Financial Education :** Receiving cashback in cryptocurrency can encourage users to learn more about cryptocurrencies, financial markets, and underlying technologies. This can contribute to a better overall understanding of modern monetary systems.

8. **Innovative Nature :** Owning a card that offers cashback in cryptocurrency reflects an innovative approach to traditional methods of reward and payment. It allows users to become acquainted with new trends and technologies in the financial sector.

9. **Opportunity to Participate in DeFi Projects :** Some cryptocurrency cashback cards allow users to participate in DeFi (Decentralized Finance) projects using the received cryptocurrencies. This can offer opportunities for borrowing, lending, or participating in liquidity pools.

Over the years, I have had the opportunity to use several of these cards personally, including the Binance card, Crypto.com card, and Plutus card. I choose not to go through the taxation step because I transfer funds directly from my personal account in fiat currency, thus avoiding any fiat-to-cryptocurrency conversion that could result in tax obligations. Furthermore, these cards can be used for cryptocurrency spending, but caution should be exercised by carefully calculating any resulting capital gains.

These cards can be used for all everyday expenses (internet, shopping, etc.) and offer cashback ranging from 1% to several percentages depending on the platforms.

- **CRYPTO.COM Card**

Crypto.com offers a range of plans to subscribe to their debit cards, each offering specific benefits and features.

Here's an overview of the different existing plans :

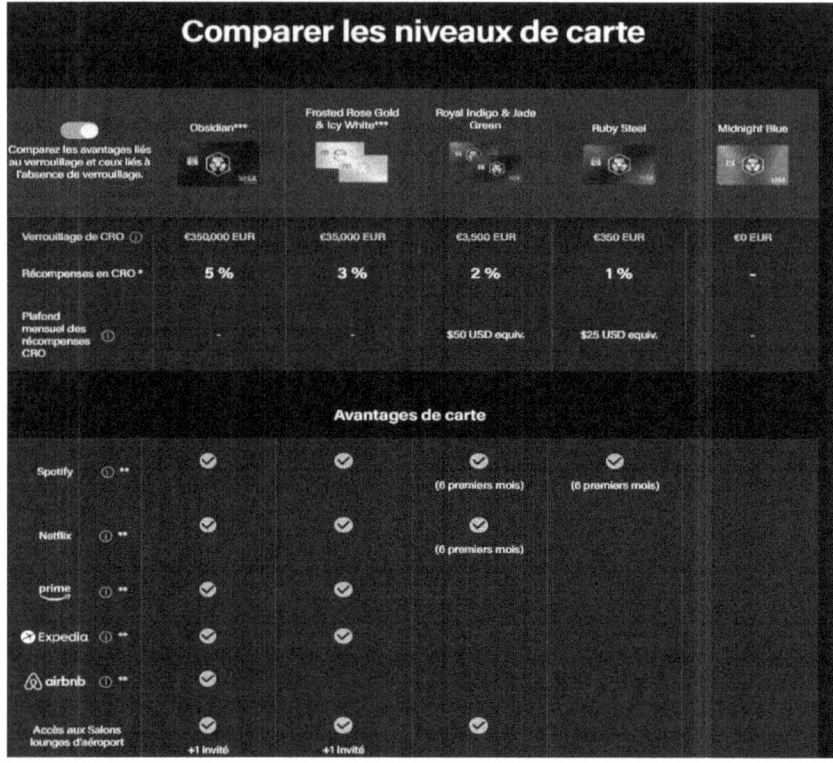

1. **Obsidian Black** : The Obsidian Black is Crypto.com's premium card. It offers a comprehensive range of benefits, such as a 5% cashback on spending, exclusive access to airport lounges, Netflix and Spotify reimbursement benefits, and much more. This card is accessible with a purchase of CRO (Cronos) for 350,000 euros (CRO must be staked for 6 months). The monthly reward cap is set at $50.

2. **Frosted Rose Gold/Icy White** : The Frosted Rose Gold/Icy White is an intermediate option offering a 3% cashback on spending, with benefits such as Netflix and Spotify reimbursements, as well as LoungeKey card access. It requires a purchase of CRO (Cronos) for 35,000 euros (CRO must be staked for 6 months). The monthly reward cap is set at $50.

3. **Royal Indigo, Jade Green**: These cards offer a 2% cashback on spending and include benefits such as Netflix and Spotify reimbursements. They require a purchase of CRO (Cronos) for 3,500 euros (CRO must be staked for 6 months). The monthly reward cap is set at $50.

4. **Ruby Steel**: These cards offer a 1% cashback on spending and include benefits such as Spotify reimbursements. They require a purchase of CRO (Cronos) for 350 euros (CRO must be staked for 6 months). The monthly reward cap is set at $25.

5. **Midnight Blue**: The Midnight Blue is Crypto.com's entry-level card, offering a basic 0% cashback on spending. No staking is required for this card.

In summary, Crypto.com offers a range of debit cards with increasing levels of benefits depending on the amount of CRO staked. Users can choose the plan that best suits their needs and preferences regarding benefits and rewards.

- **PLUTUS Card**

Comparable to Crypto.com, Plutus positions itself as a service closely tied to cryptocurrencies. At the core of its ecosystem is its own cryptocurrency: PLU. A unique feature of Plutus is its ability to be used and provide benefits without requiring direct handling of cryptocurrencies, which is also what I do myself.

Plutus, a UK-based company, has recently caught my attention, although its creation dates back to 2015.

At the heart of Plutus's offering is a debit card that features two major characteristics.

1. **Cashback**: Plutus unveils an exceptionally advantageous financial yield program: you can enjoy an outstanding 3% cashback on all your card purchases. It is important to note that this card, without requiring cryptocurrency stacking, stands out as one of the most generous cashback offers to my knowledge. The process is simple: once your card is ordered and activated, every expense you make automatically earns you a 3% cashback. This 3% cashback is paid out in the cryptocurrency "Pluton," which is PLU. After a 45-day period, you can use this amount to top up your debit card, triggering a conversion into euros. If you decide to stack PLU, the cashback percentage can even increase. It can reach an impressive 8% by stacking 2,000 PLU.

2. **Perks**: In addition to cashback, Plutus offers a range of additional benefits called "perks." These include full reimbursement of certain monthly services.

Here's an overview of the perks available in May 2023:

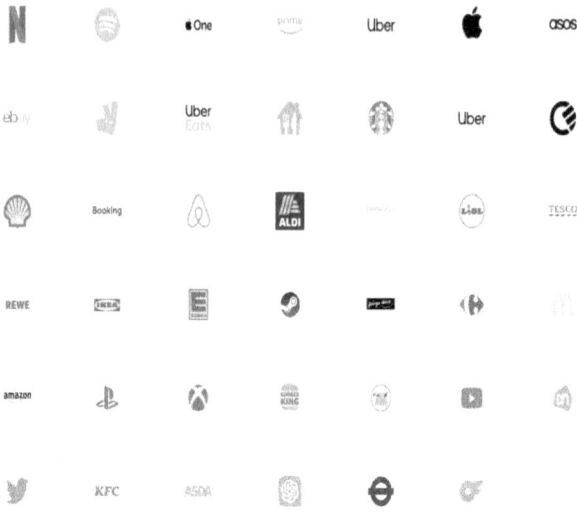

With Plutus' free plan, you can enjoy one perk every month. This includes a €10 PLU cashback for using Twitter, McDonald's, or Uber, which you can convert to euros within 45 days.

You can choose your perks for the next month by changing your perk selection. If you don't make a selection, your current perks will be automatically renewed.

You can also increase the number of your perks up to 8 by staking more PLU.

While using Plutus is free, the "Starter" plan only offers 3% cashback and one perk. Additionally, the cashback is capped at €250 in monthly spending.

Here's a summary of the key points :

- Free plan benefits:
- One perk per month (e.g., €10 cashback for Twitter, McDonald's, or Uber)
- 3% cashback on up to €250 in monthly spending
- Additional perks:
- Increase the number of perks up to 8 by staking more PLU

Considerations : Cashback is converted to euros within 45 days

You must change your perk selection each month if you want different perks

Overall, the Plutus free plan can be a good option for those who want to earn some cashback and try out a few perks without paying a monthly fee. However, if you're looking for higher cashback rates or more perks, you'll need to upgrade to a paid plan.

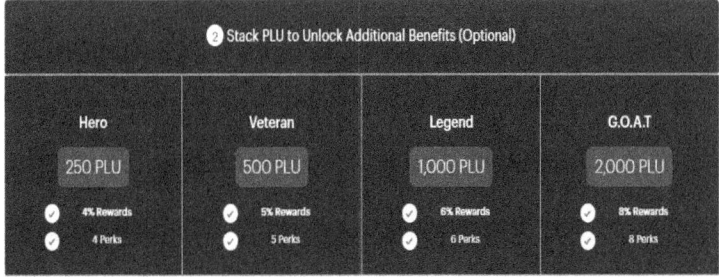

To overcome this €250 limitation, I opted for the "Everyday" plan priced

at €4.99 per month. This expanded option allows me to benefit from a second perk in addition to the cashback, which is applicable on expenses of up to €2,000 per month. To top up your Plutus account, simply make a bank transfer to the assigned RIB. Funds will be credited to your Plutus account in less than five minutes.

B. CRYPTO INDICATORS AND TIPS TO KNOW

Here are the charts not to miss if you want to understand where we stand in the cryptocurrency market:

1. BITCOIN RAINBOW CHART

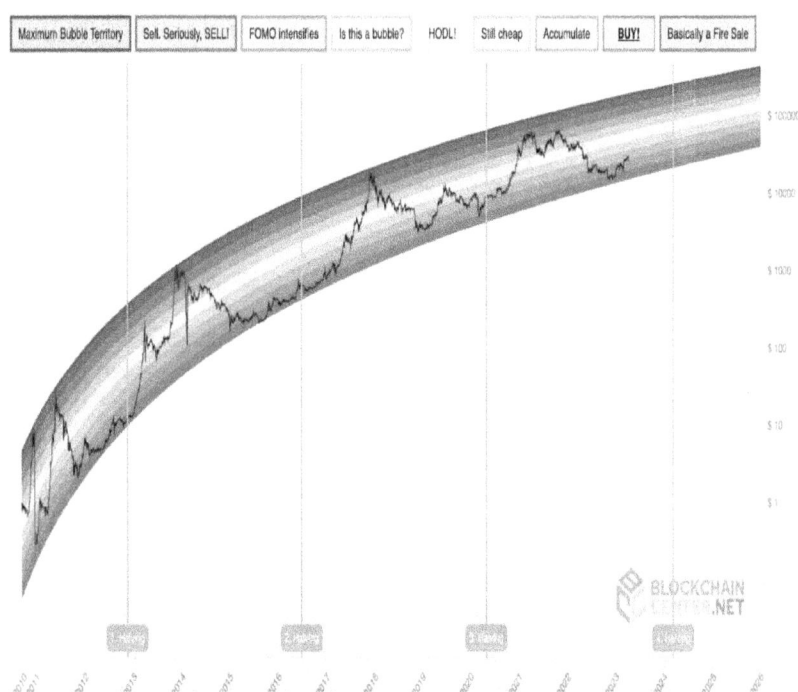

The "**Bitcoin Rainbow Chart**" is a graph that attempts to visualize the historical performance of Bitcoin using a range of colors. It is designed to help investors and observers get a general idea of Bitcoin price movements over different time periods. The chart is typically plotted using time axes (usually in years) and Bitcoin prices (usually in US dollars).

The colors of the rainbow spectrum (red, orange, yellow, green, blue, indigo, violet) are used to represent different price ranges of Bitcoin. Each range is associated with a specific color. For example, violet could represent periods where the price of Bitcoin is considered very high, while red could represent periods where the price is relatively low.

The exact meaning of the colors may vary from one version of the chart to another, but generally, bluer or violet areas represent periods where the price of Bitcoin is relatively high compared to its history, while redder or orangish areas indicate periods where the price is relatively low.

It is important to note that the Bitcoin Rainbow Chart does not provide forecasts or guarantees about future price movements. It is simply a visual tool to provide a historical perspective on Bitcoin's performance.

The same thing exists for Ethereum :

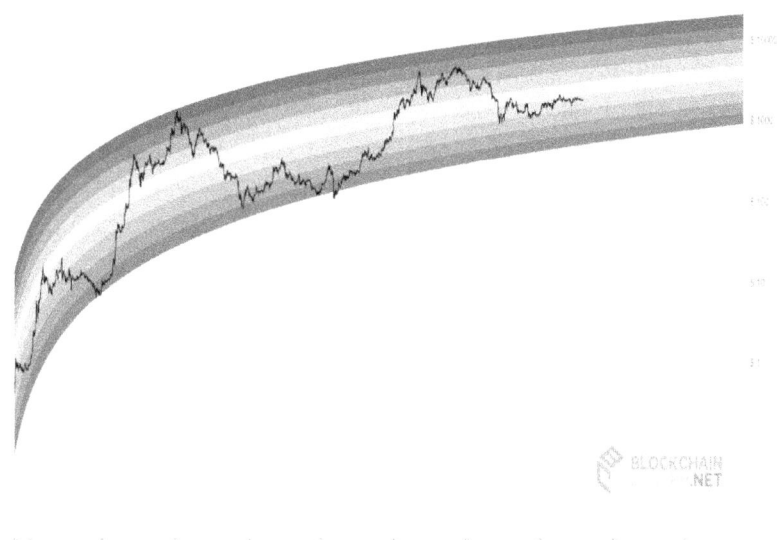

2- ALTCOIN SEASON INDEX

Imagine it as a thermometer to gauge the vitality and dynamism of Altcoins, which are all cryptocurrencies other than Bitcoin. When the Altcoin season index is high, it means that Altcoins are experiencing a period of strong growth and activity. It's as if the wind is favorable to these new crypto opportunities. This can result in significant price increases, media attention, and innovation in the Altcoin ecosystem. However, there are times when the index can be low, indicating that attention and investment are primarily directed towards Bitcoin. Altcoins may then appear to be in the background, but it's important to remember that cryptocurrency market cycles are dynamic and can change rapidly. By understanding the Altcoin season index, you'll be better prepared to navigate this complex and ever-changing universe. This will help you seize opportunities when Altcoins shine on their own and stay informed of trends shaping the exciting future of cryptocurrencies.

3-BITINFOCHARTS

On "Bitinfocharts," you have the opportunity to spot the 100 wealthiest Bitcoin wallet addresses, those holding the most significant amounts of Bitcoin.

https://bitinfocharts.com/top-100-richest-bitcoin-addresses.html

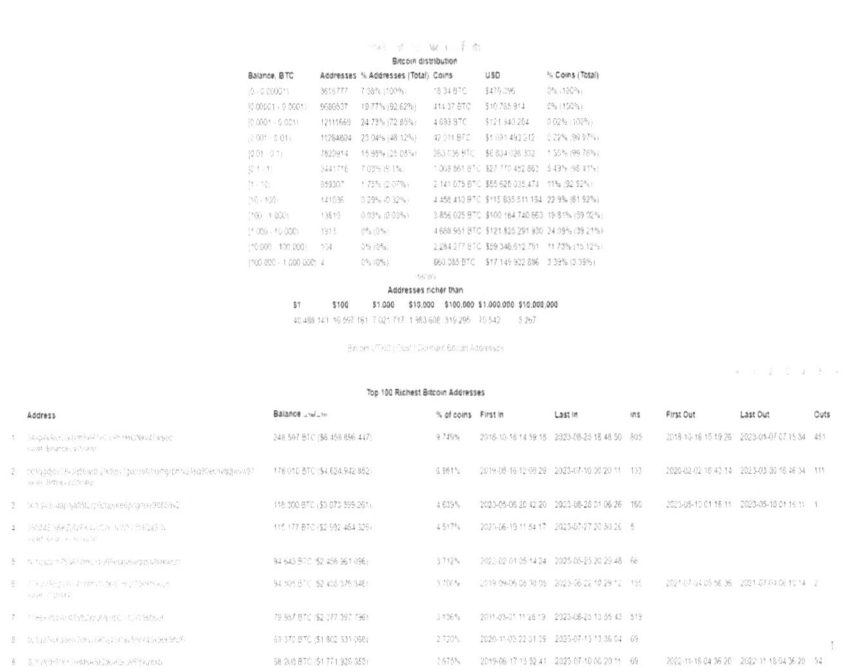

By carefully examining the top five or ten wealthiest addresses, you can discern whether the richest holders are increasing or decreasing their Bitcoin holdings. This allows you to track the movements of the most significant market whales. By acting in harmony with their purchases or sales, you can decide to buy when they buy or sell when they sell. This provides a strategic way to make decisions in the market.

4-WHALESTATS

WhaleStats is a platform dedicated to in-depth analysis of cryptocurrency portfolios, with a particular focus on Ethereum (ETH). With sophisticated tools and updated data, WhaleStats offers a unique insight into the cryptocurrency ecosystem, specifically focusing on the top 100 Ethereum wallets.

https://www.whalestats.com/analysis-of-the-top-100-eth-wallets/overview

On the "Analysis of the Top 100 ETH Wallets" page of the website, users are invited to explore a detailed view of these large-scale wallets. This analysis is an invaluable resource for investors, traders, and market observers as it allows tracking trends and movements of major Ethereum holders.

KEY FEATURES :

- **Detailed Ranking** : The site provides a list of the top 100 Ethereum wallets in terms of holdings. Each wallet is accompanied by statistics and essential information.

- **Updated Data :** The information provided is regularly updated to reflect real-time movements of wallets. This enables users to track the latest trends.

- **Graphical Visualization :** The analysis is often accompanied by visual charts that illustrate changes in the holdings of each wallet over time.

- **Trend Identification :** Users can spot holding trends, significant fund movements, and other behaviors of large Ethereum holders.

- **Investment Strategies :** Investors and traders can use this information to make informed decisions by observing the choices of the largest market players.

Here's an overview of the top ten cryptocurrencies currently held on the Ethereum blockchain:

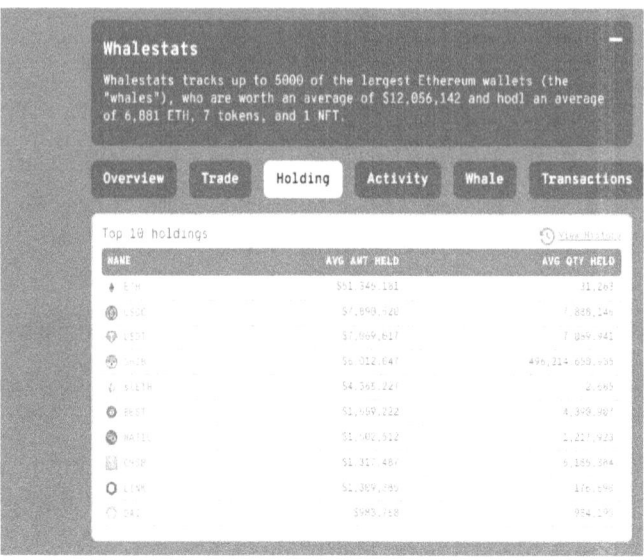

WhaleStats serves as a valuable source for those seeking to understand the movements of the most influential Ethereum wallets. This platform provides an in-depth view of major holders' evolution and their interactions with the market, thereby offering crucial insights for anyone involved in the Ethereum ecosystem.

C. BUYING CRYPTOCURRENCY FOR THE FIRST TIME

Buying cryptocurrencies may seem complicated, but I will explain the basic steps to get started as a beginner. Follow these simple steps :

1st step : Educate Yourself : Before getting started, take the time to educate yourself about cryptocurrencies. Understand what they are, how they work, and the potential risks associated with them.

2nd step : Choose a Cryptocurrency : There are many cryptocurrencies, such as Bitcoin, Ethereum, Polkadot, etc. Start by choosing a cryptocurrency you want to invest in.

3rd step : Select a Cryptocurrency Wallet : A wallet is software or a device that allows you to securely store your cryptocurrencies as we saw previously. There are online wallets, desktop wallets, and hardware wallets. Do some research to choose the type that suits you best. (MetaMask,

TrustWallet, etc.)

4th step : Sign Up on an Exchange Platform : You'll need an exchange platform to buy cryptocurrencies. Popular platforms include Coinbase, Binance, Kraken, Swissborg, Bitget. Sign up on one of these platforms and complete the necessary verification.

5th step : Verify Your Identity : For regulatory compliance reasons, most exchange platforms will require you to verify your identity by providing personal documents such as your ID.

6th step : Deposit Fiat Money : On the exchange platform, deposit fiat money (like euro or dollar) from your bank account.

7th step : Buy Cryptocurrencies : Once your money is deposited on the platform, use it to buy the cryptocurrency of your choice. Choose the amount you want to buy, confirm the transaction, and there you go, you now hold cryptocurrencies.

8th step : Transfer Your Cryptocurrencies to Your Wallet : For maximum security, transfer the cryptocurrencies from the exchange platform to your own wallet. This gives you full control over your assets.

Transferring cryptocurrencies to a wallet like MetaMask is an important step to secure your assets. Here's how to do it:

- **Install MetaMask :** If you don't have MetaMask yet, you can install it as a browser extension. You can find it on the Chrome Web Store (for Google Chrome) or on Firefox Add-ons (for Mozilla Firefox).
- **Create a MetaMask Account :** When you open MetaMask for the first time, follow the instructions to create an account. This includes creating a secure password and backing up your recovery phrase (seed phrase). This phrase is crucial for restoring your wallet in case of issues, so keep it safe and do not share it with anyone.
- **Log in to MetaMask :** Once you have created your account, log in to MetaMask.
- **Get Your Wallet Address :** After logging in to MetaMask, you will see your wallet address. This is a unique series of alphanumeric characters. Copy this address or scan the QR code if you are using a mobile device.
- **Access the Exchange Platform :** Log in to the exchange platform where you hold your cryptocurrencies. Make sure you also have access to your MetaMask wallet via another browser window or another device.
- **Withdraw Funds from the Exchange Platform :** On the exchange platform, look for the option to withdraw or transfer cryptocurrencies. Select the cryptocurrency you want to transfer to MetaMask.
- **Paste Your MetaMask Wallet Address** : Paste your MetaMask wallet address (the one you copied in step 4) into the withdrawal address field on the exchange platform.
- **Enter the Amount :** Specify the amount you want to transfer to MetaMask. Double-check that the withdrawal address is correct.
- **Confirm the Transaction :** Follow the instructions on the exchange platform to confirm the transaction. You may need to confirm via email, SMS, or two-factor authentication, depending on the security measures implemented by the platform.
- **Wait for Confirmation :** Cryptocurrency transfers may take some time to be confirmed on the blockchain. You can track the transaction status on MetaMask or on the exchange platform.

> **Once the transaction is confirmed,** your cryptocurrencies will be safely stored in your MetaMask wallet. Make sure to keep your wallet information secure and do not share it with anyone to avoid any loss of funds.

You can also use a decentralized exchange (DEX) to buy cryptocurrency: DEXs, such as Uniswap, Coswap, 1inch, or PancakeSwap, allow you to buy cryptocurrencies in a decentralized manner. Here's how it works on Uniswap, for example:

Go to the DEX website (in this case, **https://app.uniswap.org/**).

> Connect your decentralized wallet (such as MetaMask) to the DEX.
> Select the cryptocurrency you want to buy and the quantity.
> Click on "Swap" to complete the transaction.

9th step : Secure your investment : Make sure to securely store your wallet information, such as private keys. This protects you against the loss of your cryptocurrencies.

10th step : Conduct continuous research: The cryptocurrency market is volatile, so make sure to stay informed and monitor the progress of your investments.

If you have read this book carefully, here is a reminder of the 10 key elements to consider for investors looking to invest in cryptocurrencies :

1. Never invest more than you are willing to lose - it is important to consider cryptocurrency investment as a high-risk activity.

2. Do your own research before investing - it is essential to familiarize yourself with the cryptocurrency project before investing.

3. Avoid impulsive investments - decisions made under the influence of fear or excitement can be risky.

4. Diversify your portfolio - investing in multiple cryptocurrency projects can help reduce overall risk.

5. Be patient - long-term investments often yield higher returns.

6. Do not invest based on predictions - it is impossible to accurately predict the future of the cryptocurrency market.

7. Choose a secure exchange platform - a trusted platform can help protect your investments.

8. Understand fees and taxes - transaction fees and taxes can reduce returns.

9. Be aware of scams and frauds - it is important to remain vigilant and never share personal information or private keys.

10. Avoid emotion-based investments - investment decisions should be rational and based on facts rather than feelings.

By following these 10 points, investors can give themselves the best chance of success in the world of cryptocurrencies. However, it is important to remember that cryptocurrency investment always carries significant risks, and caution and diligence remain the keys to long-term success.

XI. The Final Word.

Dear reader,

As you close this book, you have embarked on a journey through the incredible story of Bitcoin, from its mysterious inception in 2009 to its rise as a global financial revolution. You have explored the essential concepts of cryptocurrencies, from blockchain technology to digital wallets, ICOs, and smart contracts.

More than just knowledge, you have gained a deep understanding of the opportunities and challenges presented by cryptocurrency markets. You have learned to navigate a constantly evolving space, make informed decisions, and manage risks. The future of cryptocurrencies is promising, but it is also complex. However, armed with this knowledge, you are prepared to face the unknown with confidence.

Beyond these words, I want to express my gratitude to you for undertaking this fascinating journey through the universe of cryptocurrencies and blockchain. Your curiosity and interest in these ever-changing subjects reflect your open-mindedness to new technologies and the opportunities they offer.

I sincerely hope this book has offered you enriching perspectives and helped you better understand the foundations, challenges, and opportunities of this exciting field. Cryptocurrencies and blockchain are transforming our society in profound ways, and you are now an informed participant in this technological revolution.

Whether you are an investor, a technology enthusiast, or simply curious, I hope this book has inspired you to explore further in this ever-evolving field. The opportunities are vast, the challenges are real, but together, we can shape a more inclusive, transparent, and sustainable digital future.

Never forget that every step you take in this field contributes to shaping the future of cryptocurrencies and blockchain. Always be vigilant, keep learning, and evolve with this growing technology.

Thank you once again for joining me on this adventure, and I encourage you to continue your exploration, ask questions, make connections, and be a part of the change.

May this digital revolution inspire you to dream big and build a better world guided by ethics, innovation, and inclusion.

Mike CryptoInvest

*** DISCLAIMER ***

I am not a financial advisor, and it is important to note that purchasing cryptocurrencies carries financial risks. I cannot provide investment advice. If you decide to invest in cryptocurrencies, make sure to conduct thorough research and consult with a professional financial advisor. Additionally, please note that purchasing cryptocurrencies is subject to market fluctuations, and past performance does not guarantee future results. We do not encourage the purchase of cryptocurrencies and cannot be held responsible for investment decisions made by users. Prudence and personal responsibility are essential when investing in financial assets.

www.ingramcontent.com/pod-product-compliance
Lightning Source LLC
Chambersburg PA
CBHW071929210526
45479CB00002B/613